# Nurturing Young Disciples

**John Buckeridge** has been the editor of *Youthwork* magazine since its launch in 1992. He is a regular speaker at Brainstormers and other youth work training events and has written several youth work curriculum books. He is involved on a weekly basis with detached youth work with his local church in Surrey.

**John Allan** is senior youth worker at Belmont Chapel, Exeter, a contributing editor to *Youthwork* magazine, and the chairman of the Evangelical Alliance Youth Ministry Committee. A well-known author, John is a regular speaker at Brainstormers and other youth work training conferences.

**Paul Borthwick** is Minister of Missions at Grace Chapel in Lexington, Massachusetts, USA and the Director of the Youth Commission for the World Evangelical Fellowship. He has written widely on youth ministry and his books include; *Feeding Your Forgotten Soul* and *Organizing Your Youth Ministry* both published by Zondervan/HarperCollins. Paul is a popular speaker at youth work training conferences.

**Tony Campolo** is professor-at-large for Eastern College, USA, and president of the Evangelical Association for the Promotion of Education which works with inner-city young people. The author of many books, Tony is a globe-trotting preacher and teacher.

**Kathy Holkeboer** is a homemaker and former staff member of Campus Crusade for Christ. She is a discussion group coordinator and teacher at Pleasantview Berean Church in Bellevue, Nebraska, USA.

**Duffy Robbins** is chairman of the department of youth ministry at Eastern College in St Davids, Pennsylvania, USA. He is well known as an author and speaker on both sides of the Atlantic.

**Dedicated to: Phil and Gill Blackledge**

The best people I know at discipling,
encouraging and empowering young people
into Christian service and leadership.

**And to: Doug Barnett**

An evangelist and former Moorlands College
tutor who has role-modelled integrity and
communication skills to many, including me.

# Nurturing Young Disciples

## JOHN BUCKERIDGE

**WITH**

John Allan
Paul Borthwick
Tony Campolo
Kathy Holkeboer
Duffy Robbins

IN ASSOCIATION WITH *YOUTHWORK* MAGAZINE

Foreword by Steve Chalke

## Marshall Pickering
*An Imprint of* HarperCollins*Publishers*

Marshall Pickering is an Imprint of
HarperCollins*Religious*
Part of HarperCollins*Publishers*
77–85 Fulham Palace Road, London W6 8JB

First published in Great Britain
in 1995 by Marshall Pickering

1   3   5   7   9   10   8   6   4   2

John Buckeridge asserts the moral right to be
identified as the author of this work

A catalogue record for this book is
available from the British Library

ISBN 0 551 02948-X

Printed and bound in Great Britain by
HarperCollinsManufacturing Glasgow

# Acknowledgements

Although I have written much of this book, I am very grateful for the crucial input of John Allan, Paul Borthwick, Tony Campolo, Kathy Holkeboer and Duffy Robbins who have contributed vital chapters.

Chapter 4 on eleven to fourteens includes adapted extracts from an article written by Peter Idris Taylor and Jan Berry which appeared in *Youthwork* magazine (February/March 1994), and is used with their permission.

# Contents

# Foreword

It comes in a glossy A4 folder. It contains eight weeks' worth of material. It deals, in neat pre-packaged sections, with the subjects of God, Jesus, the Holy Spirit, the Bible, Prayer, the Church, Giving and Witnessing. It's illustrated with cartoons. It's available from all good Christian bookstores. It costs just £3.99. What is it? You've guessed. The latest street-wise, full colour, hot off the press, *Youth Discipleship Course*.

When you think of a discipleship course, is this the first image that comes to mind? A 'helpful' series of eight half-hour sessions spent with a youth leader, the A4 folder and a Bible in the church lounge. The truth is that, at its best, this kind of material is never anything more than a valuable aid to the process of discipleship, but at its worst it amounts to nothing other than a shallow substitute for the real thing.

Discipleship is more about relationships than literature, more about learning from people you trust than from books, and more about the opportunity to get your hands dirty than sitting in the serenity of a quiet lounge being told what you should believe in order to be a model Christian. It is about being given responsibility, about being challenged, and about being made accountable. Discipleship is an *active*, not a passive, thing.

As someone who has been involved in a great deal of youth evangelism over the last fifteen years, I know only too well that it is far easier to *reach* teenagers than to *keep* them, that it's much easier to win converts than to do the thing Jesus asked us to do: to make *disciples*.

Two years ago, when I spoke at *Brainstormers*, the annual national conference for people involved in Christian youth ministry, I decided to conduct an experiment. I asked the delegates, about nine hundred of them, to stand in their places if they knew a young person who had become a Christian but had slipped away from following Christ over the previous year. I expected a sizeable response. Even so, I was not prepared for what I saw. With a handful of exceptions, the *entire* audience stood silently to their feet.

Perhaps I should not have been surprised. I became a Christian at the age of fourteen, along with a group of about thirty others, all of whom seemed to display a level of spirituality which left me feeling totally intimidated. Yet tragically, today, so far as I know, I am one of only three who are still following Christ on a day to day basis.

Humanly speaking, I survived mainly because of the efforts and influence of *one man*: Steve Flashman. Without his friendship, example, guidance, encouragement and all the openings he created for me to put my faith into practice, I would inevitably have got bored and drifted away from the commitment I had made. And I would never have had the opportunities to develop the skills and gifts which I need for my work. When I thought I could do better than him, and failed, he picked me up. He believed in me even when I blew it, and was always ready to give me another opportunity.

Later, another mentor entered my life: David Beer. Once again, I had the benefit of working alongside someone older and learning from his greater experience of life, faith and involvement in ministry. I saw him in action, copied what he did, quizzed him about why he did it, and was held accountable to him. I am constantly aware how much of what God has been able to do in me and through me over the years I owe to these two disciplers. The deepest lessons I have learnt about God, life, myself, and my faith have generally not been through books, but from these two men and others like them.

That's why I am convinced by and committed to the radical message of this book. And why I wholeheartedly commend it to you. It sets out the essential principles of mentoring and nurturing young disciples – principles which, if we are to build a healthy, vibrant church as we enter the new millennium, we cannot afford to neglect or ignore.

*Steve Chalke, Oasis Trust, June 1995*

JOHN BUCKERIDGE

# Faith Failure (1) – *Who is to blame?*

## ANDY'S STORY

Andy had enjoyed the fast-moving multimedia concert, and was surprised to be told it was organized by a church. He thought that the entertainment would be over when the speaker was introduced, but again he was pleasantly surprised. The preacher was funny and then said some things which challenged his attitudes to life. At the end, Andy went to the front to get a booklet and pray with a Christian. He didn't usually do this sort of thing. He'd always thought that religion was for wimps, so what was going on?

Along with a couple of friends who had also gone to the front at the concert, Andy was invited to a meeting in someone's house. Because he knew some others who were going, Andy decided to try it out.

He met again the person who had prayed with him, and they talked about the concert and what the speaker had said. Andy was embarrassed about being asked to give opinions and talk about God. When the leader of the group asked him if he would like to pray, he wanted the ground to swallow him up. He looked at his friends and their faces echoed his feelings. The atmosphere at the concert and this meeting in someone's home were worlds apart. Andy couldn't wait to get away.

Andy didn't attend the nurture group again. When the youth leader spotted him in the shopping precinct about a month later, Andy mumbled something about not having the time to stop and talk. Andy's decision at the concert was muddled and was formed on the basis of one fifteen-minute talk about the Gospel, half of which had consisted of humorous stories. The fact that this was never effectively followed up only compounded the original problem. Andy became a faith failure.

## DEBBIE'S STORY

Debbie had been attending church since she was two weeks old. Her parents are both heavily involved in church, on various committees, working with the Sunday school, writing to missionaries, helping clean the church rooms ready for Sunday, editing the church magazine . . . you name it, Debbie's parents do it!

What's more, their faith involves more than these activities. Often when Debbie went to the bathroom late at night she could hear her parents praying as they knelt at the foot of their bed. She knew that they loved God and that their Christian faith was at the centre of their lives.

Debbie enjoyed going to the youth fellowship. Two of her best friends went along and it was a good chance to meet and have a gossip. As for the God-thing, as she called it, Debbie regarded herself as a Christian, although she always found prayer and reading the Bible tough.

However, she firmly believed in doing good, not lying, being kind to animals and poor people, and she was a virgin even though most of her friends who were studying A-levels had 'been all the way'. She occasionally drank, but didn't smoke and regarded drugs as both stupid and dangerous.

Which was why Debbie's parents and her youth leader found it hard to believe when she got pregnant, decided to have an abortion, confessed to taking amphetamines regularly – all within two terms of attending university. What's more, Debbie insisted that she no longer believed in God.

Debbie's beliefs had collapsed very quickly once she left the immediate influence of her parents and church. Another faith failure.

The fact is that all too often we allow young people to become faith failures. When it comes to nurturing young people and seeing them effectively discipled into men and women of God, who are living radical lifestyles which reflect the value-system of Jesus, the result is all too often disappointing. Why?

When things go wrong we tend to look around for things or people to blame.

*'It's the kids' fault. They just don't care about living for God, they're selfish and only want what is going to make their life easy, comfortable and pleasant.'*

*'It's the fault of the media – newspapers, TV and film makers. Hollywood and the tabloids have corrupted our youth and seduced them with their images of easy sex and materialism. We can't compete against their billions of bucks!'*

*'It's my fault' as a Christian youthworker I should have done a better job. I didn't give them enough of my time and I didn't pray for them enough. I'm afraid that God is going to hold me responsible for their faith failure.'*

*'If only the minister and the rest of the church had got behind the youthwork, things would have turned out differently. They never financed, trained, encouraged, prayed or welcomed the kids into "their" services – it's all their fault.'*

*'It all went wrong because the big crusade evangelist didn't tell them what discipleship is all about. He sold them a cheap gospel which focused on the benefits to be gained, not the cost involved.*

*I'm not sure if they were ever really Christians and it's all the
evangelist's fault.'*

I have heard variations on all of the above and often it would seem
to be true that these factors were direct or indirect causes. But just
laying the blame at someone's or something's door is itself a point-
less exercise. What we need to do is examine in some depth the
reasons why young people fail to grow in or fall away from faith
and then prayerfully to identify strategies to reduce the casualty
rate.

Sadly it has taken the Church in general and us youthworkers in
particular too long to address the failings and seek with God's help
the remedy for the cause.

But before we do that we must first ask ourselves what is a
disciple? What are we seeking to achieve through our youth
ministry? Is a cause for failure simply the fact that our aims are
fuzzy or even nonexistent?

## What is a Disciple?

A person's last words are important. Parting messages are often
deeply significant. Those who are about to die or to emigrate tend
not to clutter up their farewells with inconsequential comments or
throw-away lines.

Jesus' last words to His disciples before He ascended into heaven
were carefully chosen: Matthew 28 records that Jesus told them to
'Go and make disciples of all nations . . .' (Matthew 28:19). This
statement makes it plain that conversion is not the end of the work
of God in a person's life. Jesus did not command His followers to
make converts but *disciples*. So what is a disciple?

The Greek word used for disciple (*mathetes*) means 'a learner',
and was used to describe a person who followed the ways and
words of a teacher and imitated his ways. *Disciple* is used in the

New Testament to describe Jesus' followers in four senses:

1  The Jews who became His followers (e.g. John 6:66).

2  The twelve apostles (e.g. Matthew 10:1).

3  All who demonstrate they are Christ's disciples by abiding in His word (e.g. John 8:31).

4  Members of the early Church as recorded by Luke (e.g. Acts 19:1).

The gospels also use 'disciple' to describe:

• People who follow a particular teaching or movement (e.g. the Pharisees, Matthew 22:16).

• Those who believed in Christ, but failed to continue to follow Him (e.g. John 6:66 identifies 'early' disciples who had turned away having found the commitment Christ calls for too difficult).

*The Applied Bible Dictionary* (Kingsway) describes discipleship in first-century Palestine thus:

Religious leaders received their training through a well-defined system. Recognized rabbis attracted disciples, who lived and studied with them. The rabbi provided support for his students; they devoted full-time to serving the rabbi and learning from him. The goal of discipleship was that the learner would not only master what his teacher knew, but also become like him in piety (Luke 6:40). The people of Jesus' time were amazed when He displayed learning 'without having studied' with a rabbi in this traditional manner (John 7:15).

So Jesus' disciples, in the tradition of the time, literally lived with him. They travelled with him, watched all he did, and listened to all he said. When Christ finished a day of public ministry, He taught His disciples privately, asking them questions and explaining what they had observed.

Along with *mathetes*, another key Greek word worth studying to reveal the true nature of what a disciple is, is *akolouthein* which means 'to follow'.

Used seventy-seven times in the gospels, almost exclusively to refer to following Christ, it is used in the literal sense (e.g. Matthew 4:25) and metaphorically of discipleship (e.g. then He called the crowd to Him along with His disciples and said: 'If anyone would come after me, he must deny himself and take up his cross and follow me' Mark 8:34).

William Barclay's *New Testament Words* (SCM) helpfully lists the common usage of *akolouthein* in classical Greek.

It is used about:

- Soldiers following their commander.

- Slaves following or attending their master.

- Obeying or following someone else's opinion or instruction.

- Obeying the laws of the land.

- Following the argument or thread of a discussion.

- Attaching yourself closely to someone in order to extract a favour.

Barclay makes the point that each of these common usages at the time can throw light on Christian discipleship.

- We follow a supreme commander.

- We should obey like a slave the commands of Christ our master.

- We should ask for guidance from Christ and be humble enough to follow His advice.

- The Christian desires to be a citizen of heaven and if he/she is to attain it, must live by its laws.

- The Christian is a learner who must listen to Christ's words.

- The Christian needs and wants the favour and grace of Jesus who wants to help and teach him/her.

Barclay encourages the reader to study the usage of the word *akolouthein* in the New Testament. Among his writings he identifies three key uses which further illustrate the nature of discipleship.

## 1 Following involves a cost

At times Jesus appears actively to discourage people from following Him until they are absolutely sure they are aware of the cost involved. That cost involves sacrifice and a cross. Following Christ means an act of surrender of one's own priorities, interests and agenda.

*The Message*, a modern paraphrase of the New Testament by Eugene Peterson (NavPress), puts in striking modern English one instance of Jesus emphasizing the cost of discipleship:

> On the road someone asked if he could go along. 'I'll go with you, wherever,' he said.
>
> Jesus was curt: 'Are you ready to rough it? We're not staying in the best inns, you know.'
>
> Jesus said to another, 'Follow me.'
>
> He said, 'Certainly, but first excuse me for a couple of days, please. I have to make arrangements for my father's funeral.' Jesus refused. 'First things first. Your business is life, not death. And life is urgent: Announce God's kingdom!'
>
> Then another said, 'I'm ready to follow you, Master, but first excuse me while I get things straightened out at home.'
>
> Jesus said, 'No procrastination. No backward looks. You can't put God's kingdom off till tomorrow. Seize the day.'
> (Luke 9:57–62)

## 2 What following Christ gives us

Following Jesus means we have Christ as our companion, guide, friend and master. It means we enjoy freedom from guilt and the fear of the reward our sins deserve. Christ's sacrifice on the cross was not for nothing – He paid the price so we could enjoy eternal life with God in heaven.

### 3 There are inadequate ways of following Christ

Barclay writes; 'These ways are not to be condemned, they are infinitely better than nothing, but they are not the best.

'At the end Peter followed Jesus "at a distance" (Matthew 26:58) . . . if Peter had kept closer to Jesus the denial might never have happened.

'On the last journey to Jerusalem the disciples followed "afraid" (Mark 10:32) . . . they feared the worst, and yet they followed Him.'

### 4 We can refuse to follow Christ

When Jesus explained the cost of discipleship the rich young ruler refused to make the sacrifice required – he couldn't give away his money, and so went away in sorrow (Matthew 19:21).

We have free will and although the Holy Spirit convicts us and can give us faith to believe, each individual has to make a personal decision to accept Christ and pay the price, or to reject Him. The story of the rich young man reminds us that the ultimate fate of those who walk away instead of following Christ is deep sorrow.

## What are we aiming at?

. . . You are slow to learn. In fact, though by this time you ought to be teachers, you need someone to teach you the elementary truths of God's word all over again. You need milk, not solid food! Anyone who lives on milk, being still an infant is not acquainted with the teaching about righteousness. But solid food is for the mature, who by constant use have trained themselves to distinguish good from evil. Hebrews 5:11b–14 (NIV)

The picture of spiritual infants growing and progressing to solid food (meat) is used, as in 1 Corinthians 3:1f, to urge believers to grow into maturity. The writer of Hebrews rebukes his readers for their lack of development.

These passages are often used in reference to nurturing new believers. But further specific guidance should be given. What specific measurable goals should we expect believers to attain and within what timespan?

There is truth in the saying, 'If you aim at nothing, you'll hit it.' So what are we aiming at?

In his excellent book, *The Mutiny of Nurture* (Zondervan), Duffy Robbins takes Paul's words to the Ephesians (4:11–16) as the basis for his suggested spiritual growth targets for new believers. From that passage, Robbins isolates four key texts:

1 'We will in all things grow up into him who is the Head, that is Christ' (Ephesians 4:15b) – converts should grow in their personal relationship with Christ.

2 'To prepare God's people for works of service' (Ephesians 4:12) – converts should understand they are called to serve.

3 'We will no longer be infants' (Ephesians 4:14) – converts should grow into a maturity of thinking and lifestyle leaving behind old attitudes and behaviour.

4 'From him the whole body, joined and held together by every supporting ligament, grows and builds itself up in love, as each part does its work' (Ephesians 4:16) – converts need to become an integrated part of the Christian community, the Church.

This blueprint is very helpful, but alongside these aims we also need clear, measurable goals. Maturity isn't an easy thing to quantify and measure. I believe both discipler and disciple, youth worker and new convert will find it helpful prayerfully to set measurable goals which if attained will help reach the general, harder to quantify or measure, aims.

The danger of introducing goals, however, is that they can become a legalistic and artificial measure of spiritual growth and maturity. This Pharisaic approach is the kiss of death and must be avoided at all costs.

However, a laissez-faire attitude is equally dangerous. In avoiding legalism, we run the risk of offering the new convert no discipline or structure to help him/her grow.

Talking and praying together with the convert and then agreeing on clear, measurable goals which will help facilitate spiritual growth is what is often required.

Some new converts are self-motivators and will be reading Scripture and spending quality time in prayer without much prompting or goal setting. With these people goal-setting could be a looser arrangement. However, many young people find the spiritual disciplines hard to get into, and the gentle coaxing structure of written measurable but attainable goals can prompt and help them.

But just as new believers should be encouraged to set goals, so too should we.

The nurture programme and the regular youth work programme should have measurable goals, prayerfully agreed as a team together, both for a term and annually.

The fact is that many youth groups have unwritten aims and goals, but the process of goal-setting can help us to identify our current aims and assess whether they are appropriate and in tune with what the Holy Spirit wants to do through us. Some youth groups/clubs I have visited have what seem to me totally inappropriate aims which the programme structure serves. Some of these are oriented on the following lines:

## Maintenance

The main aim of groups in maintenance mode is to keep their existing membership. The membership is usually made up of the sons and daughters of church members. The young people enjoy meeting their church friends at the group, but this clique is very hard for newcomers to break into and join unless the group decide to make the extra effort to be friendly and welcome them. Outside influences are seen as hostile and are resisted. Maintenance-oriented groups are common where the overall ethos of the church is also maintenance-driven, but they can also exist in mission-oriented churches if allowed to!

## Fellowship

At first glance fellowship-oriented groups are very similar to maintenance-driven ones. However, these groups are a little easier for newcomers to break into. The programme centres around activities and teaching which build trust between members and emphasize 'body-ministry' and shared experiences. The leaders usually place great store on the value of camping or other forms of residential weekends/weeks away together, which help foster togetherness. Although the leaders and group members welcome newcomers into the group they tend not to make much effort to recruit new members, or if they do, these tend to be from within the same socio-economic group as the existing members.

## Entertainment

Leaders of these groups are driven by the belief that only a high-quality programme with emphasis on fun and entertainment will continue to attract the young people. Often these groups are well run and 'professional', with a fast-moving variety of elements to the programmes. These groups are often seen by the church as being successful. Most require a large number of staff to facilitate the complicated, high-tech programme content. The young people who attend appear to be easily bored and tend to tire quickly of the latest programme innovation. Sometimes the leaders do not know all of the young people's names and the level of relationship between youth workers and young people can be superficial.

These groups were typical of many American church youth groups in the 1980s and early '90s, although many churches have rejected this model and replaced it with a more relational model. Publishers of youth ministry resources, particularly in the US, believing that this model was the future for most groups, have produced a large range of *1,000 Crazy Youth Group Games*-type books in response.

## Containment

Working with unchurched youth, mainly from working/underclass backgrounds has often resulted in the development of what I classify as 'containment-oriented' clubs. The youth workers take on the role of a warden who patrols a hall which typically has a pool and table-tennis table, table football, five-a-side football and a tuck shop. The 'wardens' spend most of their time protecting equipment and maintaining discipline and order. The club was originally launched with lofty ideals but the staff have become demotivated through lack of training, the sense that the church does not support the club, and the difficulty of building meaningful relationships with the young people, some of whom act violently towards them. Some staff are intimidated by the young people and retreat behind the tuck shop. Discipline often depends on just one or two staff members whom the kids respect.

The club may be subsidized by the local council as well as receiving church funding. Both church and council leaders may see the club mainly as a useful place to keep kids out of trouble and off the streets. Some church members/leaders demand the club has a five-minute 'talk'. This fails to communicate effectively with the youngsters who resent it intruding into the evening, and regard it as a necessary 'evil' that must be endured.

Before a group is set up, aims should be formulated. What do we want to achieve with the young people?

If it is to make an initial relationship-building contact with young people then it could be that detached youth work is the model we choose to achieve our goals.

If it is to develop existing relationships with unchurched contacts, an open youth club might be the model we choose.

If it is to explain the Gospel in a way and style they can understand and will enjoy, a six-week enquirers group may be the model.

If it is to encourage and nurture new believers we may want a nurture/house group which will then feed into a youth fellowship as the model we select.

The aim should come first and be the basis for the model we select. Too often people decide on the model or programme shape before clearly articulating the aims and goals.

## Common Reasons Why Young People Fail to Develop as New Converts

### 1 *Premature or Careless Birthing*

After over thirty hours of pain and distress my wife Alice had finally reached the last moments of labour and was about to give birth to our first child. I will never forget the moment when my son left my wife's body. He was limp and the colour of putty – he looked lifeless. He was lifted onto a towel and a tube placed into his mouth to suck out any blood and mucus. As the seconds passed and his body didn't move or make a sound I grew increasingly frantic. Although the doctor, midwife and nurses were calm I was sick with worry.

I knew that despite the care Alice had taken during her pregnancy – a good diet, avoiding alcohol or breathing in other people's cigarette smoke, all to give our baby the best chance to be healthy – it could end in disaster. Would our first-born live? Would he be damaged in some way? My eyes met my wife's in mute fear.

Moments later he breathed his first breath and within a few seconds changed colour from blue/grey to a healthy pink. Our child was born and he was healthy and well. As I held Adam Wesley Buckeridge in my arms I prayed a prayer of thanks and relief as I dedicated him to God. He thrived and quickly grew out of baby-hood into childhood.

A person's introduction to faith 'being born-again' is just as dramatic and can be just as hazardous. For as well as a healthy birth, some people are 'birthed' with inadequate care, resulting in a malformation in their faith growth.

If you introduce someone to Jesus it is both a great privilege and an enormous responsibility. A failure on your part to present the good news of Jesus in a balanced and truthful way, may result in the person making an ill-informed decision to accept or reject Christ. This problem is not restricted to personal witnessing, indeed in my opinion it is in the preached word that the lack of balance most often exists.

Preachers, evangelists, ministers, youth workers etc, who preach or teach about the benefits of becoming a Christian without spelling out the cost involved are guilty of a sin. Selling Jesus like a door-to-door salesman, where only one side of the story is told and the sale is concluded with a high-pressure 'technique', has resulted in the premature birth and subsequent damage to many people. Instead of growing and flourishing in their new faith, they falter and die because they were birthed badly.

I'm not suggesting that if a new believer falls away it is always a bad birth that is at fault. A range of other factors may have caused it, including the conscious choice of the person to reject or fail to live out his/her faith.

But all too often I have heard only half a Gospel preached which ignored the rightful claim of Christ to be our King and Master, as well as our best Friend and Saviour.

I have also heard appeals at the end of a message which were manipulative and hyped. I am not against appeals – Jesus, Peter and Paul all appealed to their hearers to respond to the message.

In the Parable of the Great Banquet (Luke 14:15–24) the master tells his servant to 'go out and *make* them come in, so that my house may be full' (verse 23). Perhaps a better word than the NIV choice of 'make' is 'compel' used by the Authorized Version. The greek word *anankazo* denotes to constrain, entreat and persuade.

The Bible commentator Matthew Henry refers to this as a compulsion 'not by force of arms, but by force of argument'.[1] The reformed commentator William Hendrikson considers the compulsion was 'by the force of loving and powerful persuasion'.[2]

At the climax of Peter's great sermon at Pentecost Luke records that 'with many other words he *warned* them and *pleaded* with them' (Acts 2:40).

The length of Peter's invitation is uncertain but the Greek tense (imperfect active) suggests he 'kept on exhorting' according to Robertson, author of *Word Pictures in the New Testament* Volume 3 (SSBSBC) 1930.

The terrific response was not due to bare doctrinal teaching alone, but due to the stimulus of Spirit-filled exhortation.

Moffatt, another respected commentator, translates the phrase: '. . . and with many another appeal he urged and entreated them.'[3] This passage supports a scriptural basis for spending a reasonable percentage of time in the evangelistic message on an appeal to believe – an invitation with a strong urging to respond.

The Acts of the Apostles and the Epistles are littered with accounts of Paul's persuasive preaching.

Some people quote 1 Corinthians 2:4, 5 as a defence against persuasive preaching and the use of evangelistic appeals: 'My message and preaching were not with wise and persuasive words, but with a demonstration of the Spirit's power, so that your faith might not rest on men's wisdom, but on God's power' (NIV).

'At first glance this suggests Paul was not a persuasive preacher.

However, Paul's aim here is to show that he did not use any illicit means with respect to either content or form . . . Paul has no objection to persuading words, on the contrary he uses them himself, but he objects to words dictated by worldly wisdom.'[4]

'We try to persuade men' writes Paul in 2 Corinthians 5:11a, but he did not believe the end justified the means. Paul worked to an ethical code of practice in his preaching – so should we all. I have written at some length on this matter because it is so important, and in my opinion, a common fault in many evangelistic meetings so that the appeal is botched.

A preacher may give no clear invitation to respond to the Gospel. Often this is through fear of apparent failure, although Scripture clearly teaches it is the Holy Spirit who convicts and gives the gift of faith to respond. But a good fisher of men will not neglect to draw in the net!

The other main fault is an unclear or unduly protracted appeal. When inviting a person to become a Christian or to find out more about what being a Christian involves, our explanation must be very clear. When the Holy Spirit brings conviction of sin, the emotions are stirred. God communicates to us as whole people – mind, body and spirit. The Gospel will provoke the mind as well as stir the emotions – therefore the person will be in a state of agitation and possibly close to tears. It is vital that our explanation of the Gospel is clear, and some phrases in the appeal part of the message may need to be repeated to ensure the person has heard correctly.

Too often people have risen to their feet, raised a hand or come to the front without having a clear understanding of what this response represents.

Just as bad as an unclear appeal is a drawn-out appeal. In a fleshly attempt to whip up emotion the appeal goes on and on, with an excited and artificial use of voice and background music designed to play on the emotions.

If God's Spirit is moving then the preacher does not need to resort to these tricks. And if it is not then any response will be artificial and not lasting anyway! So for both ethical and pragmatic reasons these overemotional and protracted appeals are wrong.

American evangelist Leighton Ford helpfully distinguishes between emotionalism and emotion. 'Emotionalism is emotion isolated, emotion for emotion's sake.' Ford goes on to say that there is a legitimate place for emotion in evangelism since 'nothing truly human lacks emotion'.[5]

But a premature or careless birthing is not the only possible cause for subsequent faith failure.

## 2  *Failure to Integrate into the Church*

A city-centre non-alcoholic bar held on two evenings a week for just three months results in the conversion of fourteen young people. The local youth worker who coordinated the project along with twelve others from a range of churches in the city prayerfully considers which church these new converts are sent to.

Just two months later only five of the original fourteen show any interest and this is restricted to attending a youth group. None attend the main church services. After a further six months just three out of the original fourteen attend a church youth group, and only one attends the all-age church worship service. A full year after the opening of the coffee bar the situation remains the same; only one out of fourteen could be said to be in any way a part of the whole community of believers. Two others are on the fringe of a youth group but could fall away at any moment. Why such a poor result?

Their conversions seemed to the experienced eye of the youthworker in charge to be genuine. Surely he wasn't wrong about all fourteen? All similar evangelistic outreach in the city was halted for six months while the situation was examined. Why was there such a high faith failure rate?

The discoveries included most of the reasons on the list

below, which I consider are the commonest causes of the failure of
young believers to be integrated into the life of the church.

### i Not a priority

For many Christian youthworkers, seeing that Christian young
people are fully integrated into the life of the church is not a high
priority.

The young people may feel they get their teaching, worship,
fellowship and encouragement from the youth group. That is their
church so they don't need the adult version.

But young people miss the dimension of community if they are
not integrated into the cosmopolitan mix of the all-ages church.
This means more than attending meetings. Taking part in meetings,
being part of the power structures of committees, serving other
members of the church, helping the church to reach into the
community around and abroad – all this and more is lost if we don't
prioritize integration and young people don't catch that vision.

### ii Church talked down

One reason for some young people having a low opinion of the
church is the fact that the youthworkers fail to encourage them to
take an active part in its life. In some cases their own dissatisfaction
with aspects of the church is communicated to the young people –
either verbally through critical comments, or through less blatant but
just as damaging inferences, jokes about the minister/leaders, etc.

The young people will quickly pick up the 'vibes' about how
youthworkers feel. This is difficult to deal with if there are justifi-
able grounds for unhappiness with the church leadership, but we
must be careful not to be negative and prejudice others.

### iii Dropped in at the deep end

Less so now, but commonly in the past a new believer was expected
immediately to swim at the deep end of church life. The new spark

of life in the convert is most often drowned by this Rambo attitude to nurture and integration.

Happily, most churches now see the need to provide nurture and care programmes which *gradually* introduce the convert to the various currents and depths of what we call church.

## iv  No genuine welcome

Sadly, some churches, while professing the desire for new converts, underneath are fearful of an influx of new ideas, fresh impetus and different faces. For them, the church is a small club with familiar faces and routines where they feel secure. Young people, or for that matter any newcomers, are regarded as a threat to the tranquillity of 'their way of doing things'. Any new faces here will soon realize they are not welcome.

## v  Instant conformity required

Even if the welcome is genuine, in some churches it is a qualified welcome. New members are pressurized subtly – and sometimes not so subtly into conforming to the status quo of the club. Often the behaviour required has little to do with the heart of the Gospel. Instead, conformity to a cultural style or attitude is at the heart of the demands made on new believers.

## vi  Boring services

Even if the welcome is genuine, and unfair, unbiblical or unrealistic demands are not made, the boring or old-fashioned content of meetings, both for all-age worship and in the youth group, will be enough to put off the new believer. Relevant and lively meetings are needed to hold the attention and really engage and involve young people.

## vii  Sore-thumb syndrome

If the new believer feels one of a kind, he/she may drop out despite everything else being right. People, especially young people, need to feel they can relate to others like themselves – it helps them to feel they belong.

For example, some inner-city churches consist of a congregation that lives in the suburbs and commutes each Sunday. A new convert from the estate where the church building stands will not feel at home if none of his neighbours worships at that church. In this instance, the answer is to win more than one person at a time, and/or for several families in the church to move in to live on the estate.

## viii  Radical convert – compromised church

Most new believers, especially young people, are radicals. They tend to read the Scripture and get excited, very often taking every text literally. They read in Acts that the believers lived communally and ask why their church is not like that. If a church is heavily compromised and failing to follow Christ's teachings the new convert will find the hypocrisy too much to cope with.

The youthworker must help channel the zeal of the new convert – not squash or dilute its energy but point out that we are all disciples and learners. While holiness must be upheld, we ourselves must be careful to avoid criticizing the speck in another's eye while ignoring the plank in our own.

New converts should be encouraged to expect high standards of the church leaders while also remembering they are fallible human beings.

## ix  Youth frozen out

Some churches refuse to allow more than a token involvement by young people in church services or committees. Church leaders who do not empower young people, or who give responsibility and power without the suitable training to facilitate the empowerment, are guilty of amputating a precious limb from the body of Christ.

All these factors can result in young people failing to become fully integrated into the whole community of the church, which in turn can result in faith failure.

I want to identify one more important factor which can lead to casualties and faith failures.

## 3 Time
There are two main time-related problems: Year-Out Syndrome and Diary Overload.

### i Year-Out Syndrome
In the predominantly materialistic and hedonistic culture we live in, what I call the Year-Out Syndrome is gathering momentum. Young people who achieve good exam results in school and win a place in university/college are opting in large numbers to take a year out of studies before college, or maybe after their first year. This year out can be to work on a worthy service project overseas, it can be a vocation-related year in industry, or it can even be a year working in a burger bar or as a nanny in order to earn money.

No problem here, you say. However, another year-out option is gaining popularity. Large numbers of young people are choosing to opt out of everything for a year. This usually means travelling abroad, making use of concessionary train, bus and air tickets to experience faraway places. This year out also involves new independence to behave or misbehave as they like. In 1994 one Euro-student rail card was actually marketed on the basis of the amount of sex in different destinations a traveller could expect to enjoy. Many other student travel operators blatantly use sex as a selling point in their 'discovery' trips.

The attitude of 'I've worked hard so now I deserve to indulge myself for a year by getting drunk, getting stoned and getting laid' is widespread. What is more, many young Christians have been infected by this hedonistic propaganda. The year out can mean a year away from the demands of discipleship and the end result is spiritual suicide.

The other side of the coin – and there is one – is that many Christians are taking a year out to serve God in a short-term mission or service project. Time For God, TIE Teams and Oasis Frontline are just three of the large number of options available. We should actively encourage young Christians to opt into God for a year instead of opting out.

But even these schemes have dangers. Some young people believe that this special year for God is 'doing their bit' and then they can go on to college and hopefully a good job earning lots of money, all with a clear conscience. So missionary societies are discovering that while they can fairly easily recruit people to serve on a short-term basis, career missionaries or people who are prepared to give a life-time of service are much harder to find.

### ii Diary Overload

The other main time-related factor which leads to many faith failures I call Diary Overload. Increasing leisure options, many of which are very time-consuming, such as computer games, plus increasingly sophisticated social activities with their peers mean many young Christians have little or no time for God, the church and the youth group.

Talking to youthworkers in some middle-class congregations I have discovered them frustrated by Christian parents who sometimes are the major culprits in causing wrong prioritization of young people's time. It is they who encourage and pay for riding lessons, music lessons, swimming lessons, dancing lessons and the million-and-one other out-of-school options on offer. Then when homework builds up and parents insist that schoolwork and revision are done, it is the church youth group/club or Christian service projects that get the elbow.

Many parents put huge pressure on their children to perform well in exams and also 'fit in' to certain social strata. A mixture of spiritual indifference and snobbery mean they can end up discouraging or even preventing a young person from mixing with unchurched 'rough' kids at the youth club or service project.

Diary Overload is not just a middle-class phenomenon, although it is more obvious there. It is a widespread problem likely to get worse as we enter the next century.

An extra contributory problem to get young people actually to attend the youth group/nurture group etc, is that parents taxi their teenagers around in the evenings for fear of crime. This puts a further strain on Diary Overload.

I partly-wrote, partly-edited this book as a contribution to the effort taking place to reduce the alarmingly high faith-failure rate among young people. Most of the rest of this book is given over to strategies to remedy the situation. But first I wanted another youth-worker to identify reasons for faith failure. A second opinion is often very helpful, and on this issue, which is so central and important to the whole of the rest of this book, I asked American youth specialist Duffy Robbins, whom I have already referred to, to high-light further causes of faith failure and/or underline problems I have so far identified. His perspective and his remedial suggestions merit careful reading.

1  *Matthew Henry's Commentary on the Four Gospels* (Hodders) 1974, page 423.
2  *Commentary on St Luke*, William Hendrikson (Banner of Truth) 1978, page 732.
3  *Commentary on Acts*, I. Howard Marshall (IVP) 1980, page 82.
4  *Commentary on 1 Corinthians*, Grosheide (Eerdmans) 1968, page 61.
5  *The Christian Persuader*, Leighton Ford (Hodders) 1966, page 122.

# Faith Failure (2) – *Tarzan Christianity*

As a young boy, one of my favourite TV heroes was Tarzan, King of the Jungle. I remember wonderful Sunday afternoons, spellbound in front of the screen, as I watched my hero swing his way through the darkest jungles of Africa, wrestling with crocodiles, laughing at snakes, talking to elephants, knocking off the bad guys and helping the good guys. Here was the kind of man a boy could look up to!

What especially impressed me about Tarzan was his ability to swing through the jungle, sailing from tree to tree with only a strong grip and a jungle vine.

I can still see him flying through forests, his bronzed muscles framed by that classic leopard-skin outfit, the whole jungle coming alive with the sound of his trademark scream (partly his means of communicating with animals, and partly a result of getting his outfit caught in the vine).

His amazing skill seemed always to be aided by a convenient vine. There was always one where he needed it, always the right length and always loose enough to release from the tree with the slightest tug.

I used to wonder about that. I wandered to the woods behind our house looking up at the treetops, suspecting that it would take more than a quick pull to launch any vines there. I worried about what might happen if Tarzan's vine were ever too long or too short. I imagined how sad it would be to see my leopard-clad hero hurtle to the jungle floor to land with a thud. These were frightening thoughts for a young child.

I think my greatest fear though was that Tarzan would just some day come to the edge of the forest and simply run out of trees. Imagine Tarzan screaming his way through the jungle . . . first to one tree . . . then to another . . . then to another . . . when all of a sudden . . . he would come to a clearing. No tree. No vine. Just a blur of flesh flying through the air. Not a pretty thought.

And yet, it is precisely that image that comes to my mind sometimes when I think about the young people we work with in our youth ministries. I can see them in my mind's eye swinging from Sunday night to Sunday night, youth meeting to youth meeting, retreat to festival.

But then, I worry, what will happen to them when they come to the clearing? What will happen when they leave our youth groups and no longer have the luxury of swinging from one treetop experience to the next? What will happen when they find themselves out there in the jungle of every-day life with all its risks and dangers?

My great concern is that what we are seeing in the lives of so many of our students is a classic case of 'crash and burn' – a plunging, groping blur of leopard skin, Bible cover and Christian T-shirt. In short we are witnessing 'Faith Failure'.

## Is There Life After Treetops?

For those of us in youth ministry the critical question is 'How can we prevent this kind of fall? How can we nurture our young people in such a way that they can survive in the jungle without experiencing the pain of faith failure?'

To be sure, it is God who begins the 'good work', and it is God who can see it through to 'completion' (Philippians 1:6; Psalm 138:8). But as youthworkers we dare not overlook the fact that our task is not completed just by getting teenage Tarzans to jump into the jungle; we need to help them land, and to stand, and to keep walking daily with Christ.

There are a number of factors that short-circuit this important work. But part of the problem of faith failure can be blamed on some imbalances in our youth ministry methods. Ultimately, the key to preventing a nasty fall is to restore a consistent balance. In this chapter, I want to develop further our examination of the common errors of imbalance in our youth ministries.

## 1  Too much arrival and not enough survival

The Christian life is a marathon. It is not about speed; it is about distance. It's not about how *fast* our kids grow; it's about how *far* our kids grow. If we want to nurture a faith that does not fail in our young people, we need to focus on strategies that encourage survival and not just arrival.

There is nowhere in Scripture where we are called to make Christians. Our mandate is to make disciples (Matthew 28:19; 2 Timothy 2:2). Only God can make Christians. Only disciples can make disciples.

The problem is that there is more excitement in the arrival than there is in the survival. Storming the beachhead is exciting. Fighting it out in the trenches to maintain your hard work – that's just hard work. Witnessing Lazarus's raising from the dead – that's a miracle. Helping Lazarus to strip away his grave clothes after four days of death – that's just gross, smelly work.

There are hugs and kisses and animated conversation when the guests first arrive. Who wouldn't want to focus their ministry on that end of the equation? After a few days of sharing the bathroom and cleaning up someone else's mess, we begin the mundane work of life in a shared community. That's not quite so exhilarating.

So much of our ministry effort is focused on helping young people to 'become Christians' that we have lost sight of our central God-given mandate. Our task in youth ministry is not just helping kids to become Christians;* it's helping kids BE the Christians they've BECOME.

## 2  Too much childish faith and not enough childlike faith

It's too bad that real life is not a flannelgraph. It would be so much easier if we could reduce all the hassles, temptations and questions of life to a few cut-out felt figures. But real life doesn't always match the Sunday school simplicity of four and five figures clinging to a flannel background.

When children are young and thinking in a concrete way, it is a

---

* Our discipleship mandate does not allow us to be mute with our testimony for Christ. Obviously, we are commanded to be witnesses for Christ (Acts 1:8). Scripture gives us a clear evangelistic call. I worry about pitting 'discipleship' versus 'evangelism' as opposing goals. Evangelism is the first stage in the process of discipleship. No one has ever been discipled who was not first evangelized.

We have all met 'discipleship snobs' who talk about evangelism and outreach as if it were a lower life form of ministry. 'I don't have the time to mess around with young people who aren't interested in doing something radical for Jesus! I didn't get into the ministry so I could have fun and games.'

Standing on the beach that day (Luke 5:10), Jesus looked squarely into Peter's eyes and said, 'From now on you will catch men.' Some of us have heard this phrase in one form or another and we know how the adventure of that evangelistic call can stir our hearts to 'leave everything and follow'.

And yet as a fisherman, Peter knew that the actual joy of hauling in the net was only part of the job. There were nets to mend, and nets to wash, there was bait to set, and boats to repair, and after all that, long nights on the boat waiting for the fish to come.

Imagine Peter complaining that he was finished with 'all-nighters', that he had more important things to do than sit in a boat and wait for the fish to come, that this business of fishing is too important to waste time with 'fun and games'. Let's just face it. It takes two things to catch fish: bait and patience. Whether we like it or not, fishing for men will always involve both (and it may occasionally require an all-nighter or two). That's the evangelistic task.

On the other hand, no fisherman in his right mind continues to catch fish without giving some thought to how he will preserve them and keep them fresh. Otherwise, at the end of the day, all he has to show for his labour is a big boat filled with smelly, dead fish. Big catch. Big deal!

We are called to make disciples. That does not mean we can make light of the evangelistic mission of the gospel.

fairly simple matter to get them to sing, 'Jesus loves me, this I know; for the Bible tells me so.' But as these children begin to move into early teen years, new questions emerge. It's a jungle out there. We hack a path around some of these questions during their younger years, and rightly so. But there comes a point at which the questions and dangers of the adolescent jungle are too many and too thick.

Doubt is a predictable part of adolescence. As young people begin to think abstractly (see chapters 4 and 5) life becomes less 'safe and protected', and they encounter episodes of struggle and doubt. These questions are intensified by different events like the breakup of the family, the loss of a friend or the emergence of faith questions that don't fit so neatly on the flannelgraph. Some young people make it through this thick undergrowth of questions with their faith intact and strengthened. Others end up getting lost in the jungle.

The Apostle Paul alludes to just this part of the adolescent safari when he writes, 'When I was a child, I talked like a child, I thought like a child, I reasoned like a child; when I became a man, I gave up childish ways' (1 Corinthians 13:11). What Paul seems to be saying is that spiritual maturity involves giving up a childish faith that believes in easy answers and holding tight to a childlike faith that trusts the Father even when there do not seem to be any answers.

'Putting away childish reasoning' means nothing less and nothing more than helping students to forge a path through the jungle, marked, not by simple, easy half-truths, but durable, biblical hard-truths.

That doesn't mean that we are in any sense to attempt to explain away the wonder and mystery of God. What it does mean is that we help the young people to come to grips with the fact that just because God is good and loving does not guarantee us safety from all unpleasant experiences of life.

Faith failure happens when we root students in a nice, clean, childish flannelgraph faith instead of the childlike trusting faith to which Jesus calls us (Matthew 19:13–14).

| **CHILDISH FAITH** | **CHILDLIKE FAITH** |
|---|---|
| Good Christians don't have pain and disappointments | God uses our pain and disappointment to make us better Christians |
| God helps those who help themselves | God can only begin to help those who admit their own helplessness |
| God wants to make us happy | God wants to make us holy |
| God always answers prayers | Sometimes He answers with 'No' or 'Wait' |
| Faith will help us always to understand what God is doing | Faith will help us to stand under God's sovereignty even when we have no idea what God is doing |
| The closer we get to God, the more perfect we become | The closer we get to God, the more we become aware of our own sinfulness |
| Mature Christians have all the answers | Mature Christians can wrestle honestly with tough questions because they trust that God has the answers |
| Good Christians are always strong | Our strength is in admitting our weakness |

## 3  Too many meetings, and not enough memories

Have you ever stopped to consider that people like Philemon, Timothy, Aquila, Priscilla and Epenetus (Romans 16:3, 5a) never had a youth group? So far as archaeologists can discern, there were no water-balloon fights or youth rallies in the first-century church.

On the other hand, experience teaches us that what really shapes values and perceptions are those vivid memories that we carry with us through life. Our lives are shaped, not by meetings, but by memories. We remember what we saw with our own eyes, what we felt with our own hands, and what we heard with our own ears.

Isn't that basically Paul's appeal to Timothy in 2 Timothy 3:10–11? 'You, however, know all about my teaching, my way of life, my purpose, my faith, my patience, love, endurance, persecutions, sufferings . . . Yet the Lord rescued me from all of them.'

Paul is saying that one of Timothy's greatest weapons as he plies his way through the jungle of real life are his memories. His walk with Christ is bolstered not by the meetings he went to, or the sermons he heard, or by the studies he took part in – all of those were important. But what carries him on the long haul are his memories of what he experienced on his journeys with Paul.

One of the ways that we can steady young people for the long haul is to make our youth groups a place of vivid memories. We need to think of ourselves not just as 'programme directors', but as 'memory makers'.

But how do we do that? The average church service is not marked by parishioners who leave their services wide-eyed and dazed, muttering, 'Wow, that was unforgettable!'

When we think about what makes a memory memorable, it's really quite simple. It boils down to a combination of some of these elements:

- the element of SURPRISE

- the element of CHANGE

- something that is NEW or UNIQUE

- a high degree of EMOTIONAL INTENSITY (positive or negative)

- a PERSONAL experience

- an element of RISK

- meaningful RITUAL or CEREMONY

- a RARE occurrence

The question that we must ask ourselves as youthworkers is

'To what degree, if any, are these elements present in my youth ministry?'

I suspect that many of us would have to admit that we may be directing well-organized, well-attended, (perhaps) well-funded youth programmes. But the majority of what we do is thoroughly forgettable.

To do a quick survey of your own youth ministry, fill in the chart with the last five youth activities that you've had in your youth group. Now go through and check off which elements were present in the various activities.

| ACTIVITY | Surprise | Change | New | Intensity | Personal Experience | Risk | Ceremony | Rare |
|----------|----------|--------|-----|-----------|---------------------|------|----------|------|
|          |          |        |     |           |                     |      |          |      |
|          |          |        |     |           |                     |      |          |      |
|          |          |        |     |           |                     |      |          |      |

Most of us go to enough meetings of various types to know that they are seldom helpful and usually easy to forget. But a wise youthworker will give his students a vast reservoir of memories, an unforgettable heritage of God at work in the ups and downs of life shared together. Faith failure doesn't happen because our students have not been to enough youth meetings. Faith failure happens because young Timothys cannot draw upon vivid memories of God at work in their lives.

## 4  Too much 'come forward' and not enough 'press onward'

The next reason for faith failure is rooted not so much in what young people reject when they walk away from the faith as in what they embrace when they walk into the faith. They embraced Tarzan Christianity because some well-meaning youthworker talked more about swinging through the trees than about walking through the jungle.

One of the oldest and most basic principles of youth ministry is this: 'What we win them with is what we win them to.' If we win young people to Christ by promising them Fantasyland, we should not be surprised when they balk at going on the Jungle Hike. An honest portrayal of the gospel message has got to include the message of Jesus as Saviour and the message of Jesus as Lord.

In over twenty years of youth ministry I have discovered it is relatively easy to get teenagers to say 'Yes' to Jesus. What is difficult is getting them to say 'No' to those things in their lives that are not Jesus. And yet, any genuine 'Yes' always has at its heart a genuine 'No'. I fear that we are sometimes so eager to have young people come forward and accept Jesus that we downplay the more difficult message of pressing onwards to obey Jesus.

This isn't a failure of faith. It's a failure to communicate the faith honestly and fully. If we win students to a Christianity with all the treetops and swinging, we should not be surprised that they shy away from the challenge of living out the faith on the jungle floor.

## 5  Too much instruction and not enough direction

I've been involved lately in intense one-on-one ministry with a teenager. We have spent long hours together, some of it in the middle of real trial, sometimes with heated conversation, sometimes wondering if we might actually be accomplishing anything at all. There have been hours of instruction, honest confrontations, earnest rebuke and even some tears along the way. It hasn't been easy. But I am committed to the process because I want my teenage daughter to learn to drive safely.

Sometimes after her lesson is over and we are safely back at the house, we will laugh about some of the conversations that unfolded in the heat of the lesson.

'Dad, why did you grab the steering wheel like that?'

'Because, sweetheart, it didn't look as if the elderly lady was moving fast enough to dodge us . . .'

Or, 'Dad, you didn't have to pull the handbrake. I saw the tree; I was going to stop.'

'Yes, Erin, I know you saw the tree. It was directly in front of us. And, I know we were going to stop. But remember, the object here is to stop without going through the windscreen.'

There is some risk involved in this process. It isn't always completely pleasant for either of us, and there are awkward moments along the way. But, in the course of these lessons I have discovered something very profound: People do not learn how to drive by going to classes and watching films on highway safety. Nor do they learn by having an instructor who stands in the driveway and yells his instructions from a safe distance. The only real way to help my daughter travel the road safely is by getting into the car beside her and giving her, not just instruction, but direction.

What she needs from me is not another study in driving but an in-car demonstration. Jesus didn't say 'I can teach you the truth'. He said 'I'm it'. 'I am the way, the truth, and the life' (John 14:6). This was not just the Word become word, this was the Word become flesh.

Too often we seek to do youth ministry from a distance – we try to turn discipleship into a classroom study or a Sunday school lesson. We approach disciple-making as if we were some kind of youth ministry lifeguard who sits above this adolescent swimming pool, and our job is to blow the whistle and yell safety instructions from a distance.

But you don't keep young people from going under from a distance; you get in the water with them. You tolerate the splashing, the wetness, the loss of your nice warm place in the sun – and you offer direction as well as instruction.

A lifeguard in the water is worth two in the chair and a dad in the car is worth ten in the driveway. Some of our young people experience faith failure simply because they don't have anyone who will give them an up-close, one-on-one, in-car demonstration. The next chapter unpacks the need for relational youthwork further . . .

JOHN BUCKERIDGE

# Relational Youthwork

A young person does not develop and grow into a mature man or woman of God in isolation; it almost always happens within the context of a relationship. From the first pre-evangelism contact, relational youthwork should be the hallmark of our approach.

I had met Gary every week since we began detached youth work on his estate two months earlier. He was friendly but slightly aloof, would chat with the team briefly but then slope away with his friends. Tonight as we approached the group of sixteen-year-olds standing by the chip shop he seemed surprised to see us.

'You're here again,' he said. I wasn't sure if it was a statement or a question. 'Is this your last week then?'

'No,' I replied, 'we'll be back next week and the week after.'

'So, two more weeks, then?'

'No, we'll keep coming here as long as we keep meeting young people.'

'Yeah, but how long for?' repeated Gary.

'We're here for good, Gary,' I insisted. 'This isn't just for a few weeks or a couple of months; the team are committed to this estate for a long period of time – years.'

The penny dropped and Gary changed. He talked to us, he listened to us, he laughed with us, we spent hours with his 'gang' of mates, we became part of his group, we became friends. Gary's perception of the church and the detached youthwork team had been that we would make a short-term effort and then go away. On that basis he wasn't interested in being friends and spending time with us.

Sadly all to often the well-meaning evangelistic efforts of the church to reach unchurched people is based on a short-term effort. A special mission, a month-long summer club, a week of special events – and then guilt assuaged, the church retreats back into its spiritual ghetto for another year.

Compare this with the approach of the Master. He spent more time outside the synagogue ministering to people than inside. God chose not to appear in a cloud and preach to the human race from a distance. Instead he became one of us and identified with the joys and struggles of everyday life. His style can best be summed up in the one word – incarnational.

## Incarnational Ministry

Paul sums it up well in Philippians 2:

> He (Christ) had equal status with God but didn't think so much of himself that he had to cling to the advantages of that status no matter what. Not at all. When the time came, he set aside the privileges of deity and took on the status of a slave, became human! Having become human, he stayed human. It was an incredibly humbling process. He didn't claim special privileges. Instead, he lived a selfless, obedient life and then died a selfless, obedient death – and the worst kind of death at that: a crucifixion. (Reprinted with permission from The Message)

Jesus identified with us completely by becoming human and by living among us.

The Greek word for communicate is *koinos*, which means 'to have all things in common'. From this root we get the word; *koinonia* which means, 'communication, fellowship, participation with'. The implication of this definition is simple. Effective communication happens when we understand the language, culture, possessions, value systems etc. of the community which the person belongs to.

That is one reason why in each issue of *Youthwork* magazine, which I edit, we devote two whole pages to youth culture update and analysis. It's not a case of being trendy or hip, but knowing the trends in local and national youth culture helps us communicate and understand.

In one South London church a newly employed full-time youthworker spent most of his first six months just discovering the intricacies of the various local youth cultures. Ignorance of youth culture leads to a lack of cultural relevance and harms communication.

Attempting to communicate to young people from a distance means our message is distorted and they can interpret the message in a way which is totally different from the original intention.

John Dettoni in his excellent book *An Introduction to Youth Ministry* sums this up well:

> Incarnational youth ministry functions as Christ did: forgetting the prerogatives of adulthood and becoming identified with youth without actually becoming just like youth. This means taking the role of servant to youth, becoming an adult for youth without taking on all their characteristics. It is so identifying with youth that one can feel their hurts, know their minds, and predict to a certain degree what they will think, feel and do. It means enfleshing Christ to youth: showing in our very being (words, actions and attitudes) what Christ continually shows to us of himself.[1]

Jesus was frequently criticized for the company he kept. The Pharisees were not slow to point out that he appeared to prefer to be with 'tax collectors and sinners' (Matthew 9:11). Luke records in his Gospel that when Jesus announced he was going to stay in Zacchaeus's house those who heard started grumbling; 'What business does he have getting cosy with this crook?' (Luke 19:6).

Jesus identified with the people he wanted to reach.

## Identification

In an area where I did detached street work, a series of thefts and vandalism had aroused the anger of the local residents and the local business community against the young people whom they blamed. The owner of the local petrol station was particularly fed up after several consecutive nights of incidents which included the discharge of fire extinguishers and stealing from his forecourt shop. After the theft of a bar of chocolate, following this series of petty crimes, he completely lost his temper. Meanwhile unaware of this latest incident the detached team including myself were chatting with a small group of youngsters nearby. I was smiling and talking when suddenly Brian, the petrol station owner, approached. Standing inches from my face he began to shout and curse at me.

'What do you think you're laughing at; think it's funny do you?'

Taken aback I looked around for a clue to explain this verbal attack while Brian continued his torrent of swearing and hate.

'I'm f—ing fed up with this lot stealing my stock and frightening my customers away, and you're just f—ing encouraging them to come out, aren't you?' He emphasized his points by jabbing me hard on the chest with his forefinger. His eyes and the veins on his neck bulging, he was taking his temper out on me.

'I've f—ing had enough, do you f—ing hear? There's going to be some f—ing broken bones around here.' Then pointing to a policeman who had come on the scene he announced that the shopkeepers were going to form a vigilante band to mete out some instant justice.

By this stage several of the youngsters were whispering into my ear suggestions such as: 'Get the first one in' . . . 'Give him a dig' . . . 'Kick him where it hurts' . . . 'You can't let him talk to you like that.'

With my stomach muscles tensed for the punch I thought was likely to come, I tried to calm Brian down and explain that our purpose for being there was to help, not inflame the situation. Eventually Brian stopped shouting and walked back across the forecourt to talk to the policeman.

Later, along with another team member, I approached Brian and the policeman and tried to explain more about our purpose and aims.

'There's no excuse for their behaviour,' was the constable's contribution, while Brian just wanted the kids to go somewhere else. I noticed over my shoulder that two of the youngsters had walked over and were listening in on our conversation, presumably to check that we were not betraying confidences.

Later the peer leader of the group of youngsters asked me a series of questions which included; 'Why didn't you hit him? Were you afraid?' 'Why do you come here and get all this bother?'

Following that incident, our whole team noticed a change in the group's attitude towards us. We had faced the sort of anger and threats they regularly received. Under pressure we had neither resorted to violence or 'grassed them up' (betrayed them). In short, we were identified with them.

I am not suggesting that you engineer such a situation, but if you spend time with a group of people, opportunities for identification with them will be sure to arise.

But identification has a price. You can expect criticism and misunderstanding from those you might expect to support you, even if you take care to communicate your purposes. What puzzled and angered the Pharisees was not just that Jesus mixed with tax-collectors and prostitutes but that he enjoyed being with them. Christ loves sinners and you and I need his love in our hearts for those we seek to identify with – not see them as 'pew fodder' but precious lives Christ died for.

I didn't enjoy the experience with Brian, or the other occasional threats, violence, abuse, misunderstanding and isolation which anyone who works with unchurched youth will meet from time to time. But rather than shun these prickly encounters I have learned they can be used for good.

Too few of us really understand the difficulties and problems which face those we seek to evangelize.

Back at the petrol station incident when the policeman blithely said, 'There's no excuse' for their thieving and vandalism, I was acutely aware of the tough situations facing many of the youngsters. One girl in the group had a large bruise on her cheek and that evening her father had visited the hospital casualty department to have an X-ray on his knuckle. I also wanted to tell Brian and the policeman about the lad who was paid by his mother's boyfriend £2 each night to stay out of the house until 10p.m. Or about another girl in the group who told a member of the team in a matter-of-fact voice that her stepbrother had raped her a fortnight ago. I didn't say anything because I would have broken confidences and besides, Brian and to a lesser extent the policeman, probably would not have been interested. I never cease to be amazed at the reaction of authority figures to teenage crime. Blame it on the teachers, social workers or the kids are the usual reactions. But what about the parents and what about the social deprivation of the area, unemployment, bad housing, and for that matter, the indifference of the church?

Identification with those you work with means more than sympathy; it leads to empathy – weeping with those who weep and laughing with those who laugh. *Feeling* the ups and downs, the joys and sorrows of young people is what I believe youth work is all about.

# Relevant Communication

Another consequence of Jesus' close contact with those he wanted to communicate with meant that he knew the everyday incidents that would best illustrate his teaching. Stories about sheep, towers falling over, harvests and a poor widow seeking justice appealed strongly to his audience.

The challenge for the Christian youthworker is to find the cultural keystones of local youth. Sometimes they will be picked out of the local newspaper, some may relate to popular song lyrics, but one thing is sure – the parables which worked in first-century Palestine need to be re-encultured. It is little use telling a story about a lost sheep in an urban situation and expecting the same reaction as Jesus got from his audience.

It will be useful if difficult to consider the exercise at the end of this chapter which will stretch you to find ways to translate abstract theological concepts into concrete stories which unchurched young people can relate to. The themes Jesus chose to communicate will still hold the attention of anyone today. Just consider some of the subjects he covered:

- Anger

- Death

- Criticism

- Doubt

- Fear

- Greed

- Hate

- Happiness

- Honesty

- Hypocrisy

- Justice
- Kindness
- Knowledge
- Lust
- Marriage
- Money
- Parents
- Prayer
- Revenge
- Tax
- Trust
- Wisdom

That is a sure-fire list to interest and engage young people today. By drawing on the common experiences of the people, Jesus held their attention and communicated with them through their needs, problems and questions.

What is more, Jesus asked more questions than he provided answers! Around one hundred and fifty questions are recorded in the Gospels. Also when he told parables he usually only provided his closest followers with answers as to their meaning. The rest were left to puzzle them out for themselves.

Close your eyes and imagine the scene following one of his parables. The people start discussing it, dissecting it, suggesting what the story meant, generally engaging in heated debate.

This was no dry and stuffy sermon – Jesus posed questions and told provocative stories to get the people thinking for themselves about matters of theology.

I believe that our task is the same – we should be acting as catalysts, providing the tools and ingredients for truth discovery and then lighting the blue touch paper and stepping back! Scenarios, role play, discussion and debate will allow the young people to explore and articulate truth. We can help channel that explosive reaction through timely intervention without always having to resort to the lecture-style sermonizing where we take control and leave the youngsters as, at best, listeners, at worst, bored non-listeners.

Our choice of stories, role plays and scenarios to encourage debate and discussion will be guided by our relational style of work. Spending time with a group of people means we learn about their lives. We can then use common experiences as word pictures, discussion triggers and for questions.

## People Not Programmes

As we spend time with, listen to, identify and build relationships with young people, understanding, insight and opportunities to share Jesus' love will come.

I believe that the quality of our literature, venues, training, and programme content in youth ministry needs to be good, but much more important than all these is that we build a relational ministry, where people count more than programmes.

Gary was interested in relationship. He couldn't be bothered to get to know a bunch of Christians who he thought would be in and out of his estate in a short time. And there's the rub – time. We need to spend time being with young people, time in their territory, not judging them, but being with them.

It takes time to get to know people individually. But if the church is effectively to reach and keep the current generation of young people, one of the vital ingredients is going to be time to build meaningful relationships.

The team I was working with spent hundreds of hours with Gary, Mark, Terry and the others in that small group over a period of four years. They are fully grown adults in their mid-twenties now, but I still hear from them occasionally.

It took three years before Gary and Mark felt ready to make a decision about Christianity. It had taken that long patiently to tell them about the gospel and talk through the issues and implications. Many things had to be repeated time after time, but three years later Gary and Mark encountered God.

Darren James is a detached youthworker who lives and works on the Blackbird Leys Estate in Oxford. Darren is one of a growing army of Christian youth workers who believes in incarnational youthwork. He has invested years of his life working with a group of young people and their families on an estate which hit the headlines a few years ago because of its problems which included 'joyriding'. Walking with Darren in Oxford it seems that everyone wants to stop and say hello. He is well known as an advocate of young people. He carries a mobile phone so he can be easily contacted by the police if they need him at the police station to act as the 'appropriate adult' in an interview.

Darren cares about people as individuals and in groups. But this takes time. All too often the Church looks for fast results, quick conversions and changes in behaviour. But generally, God's Spirit chooses to work through relationships and time must be allowed for young people to learn about the good news and then to live it out. This process of faith happens within the context of relationship.

The Bible makes it clear that our job is to be heralds of the good news. I believe our role as Christian youthworkers is to care about the whole person and through a holistic ministry and relational friendship provide sufficient information to equip a person then to make an intelligent decision about Christ. It is the job of the Holy Spirit to convict and convert, not ours.

But all too often unchurched young people reject Christianity through ignorance and learning only half-truths. They haven't actually rejected Christ, just the parody of the faith they have seen on TV, or the glimpse they have had at school or from a rare visit to a christening, wedding or funeral. Our job is to expose them to the full gospel of Jesus Christ, and that cannot be done in a day.

It can be very painful when after much time, effort and input a person decides to reject the claims of Christianity, or acknowledges the truth of the gospel but decides he/she is not prepared to become a disciple of Christ.

After three years with Jesus one of the disciples betrayed him to his enemies for money, one used foul swear words to convince people that he wasn't one of the disciples, and the rest, except for one ran away and deserted Christ at the hour of his greatest need. But, though often bickering and frequently forgetting Christ's commands and guidelines, the twelve disciples were the foundation stone on which Christ built the church.

Jesus must often have been disappointed by the disciples' reactions to problems and their slowness to learn. But he persisted and did not reject any of them. Instead he spent quantity and quality time with the twelve and other extended groups of followers. Some were to reject his teachings as too hard. But for all of them he was there among them, on view to be scrutinized and imitated.

Veteran American youthworker Wayne Rice argues that it is the job of the Church to 'surround children and young people with Christian adults they can look up to and model themselves on . . . You don't learn how to be an adult from other kids. You only learn how to be an adult from other adults. But where are they?'[2]

To learn what it means to be a Christian a young person needs to be exposed to living examples of Christianity in action. This applies just as much *after* any decision is made to follow Christ as *before*.

In a later chapter we will consider the poor standard of post-war nurture which has been offered to new young converts. The high casualty rate of these fledgling believers has forced the Church to reappraise the way it follows up these people and the aftercare structures in many churches is now much improved.

But before we rush headlong into suggested remedies to the high faith failure rate we must consider other factors which should colour our responses. Crucial to this is 'knowledge' about the young people we are working with and then allowing that knowledge to influence how we communicate with them

What is the typical worldview of a thirteen-year-old? What is it like to be fifteen and terrified of failing to live up to the expectations of one's parents? What are the current educational, musical, cinematic and advertising trends? What are the typical hopes, dreams, values and opinions of young people today?

We need to find answers to these questions if we really care about discovering what shapes their beliefs.

1  *Introduction to Youth Ministry*, John M Dettoni (Zondervan) 1993, page 22.
2  *Youthwork* magazine October/November 1994, page 23.

# The World of the Eleven- to Fourteen-Year-Old

Kirsty, like other modern thirteen-year-olds is an inch taller than teenagers twenty years ago and enjoys dramatically improved dental health than her parents' generation. However, she suffers from asthma and finds unbearable the smog of car-fume pollution in the city centre.

Like the majority of eleven- to fourteen-year-old girls she reads *Smash Hits* and *Just 17* magazine.[1] The agony aunt columns in *Just 17* and other teen mags are her main source of information about sex. Most nights she fits an hour of homework into a five-hour mix of watching TV, listening to music in her bedroom and phoning or visiting friends.

Having eaten his packed lunch of a sandwich, crisps and chocolate, washed down by a can of Cola, fourteen-year-old Danny has a difficult choice – should he play football in the twenty minutes left in the school lunch break or sit with two of his best mates who have a copy of the latest issue of *Viz*.[2] The crude sexist and often racist humour in this supposedly adult-only comic is read by over a quarter of eleven- to fourteen-year-old boys, making it even more popular with male pre-teens than computer magazines.[3]

Danny knows quite a lot about sex. Much of it comes from reading his sister's magazines, or from '18' certificate videos he has watched at his friend's house. He is dismissive of the sex education he got from school. On his fifteenth birthday he smoked a spliff (cannabis cigarette) for the first time 'to celebrate'. He reckons that buying drugs is easier in his neighbourhood than buying alcohol.

Children and young people are having to face up to adult pressures and concerns at an even younger age, a phenomenon which has spawned the tag 'adult-teens'. Surveys suggest that the number of young people who regard their childhood as a time of fun and games has shrunk to a new low with some twelve-year-olds already worrying about getting a job when they leave school. A lifestyle survey of six hundred young people in 1994 identified just 3 per cent whose lives still mirrored the traditional image of young people who live carefree fun lives.[4] 'Childhood will just be adulthood at a younger age,' comments social psychologist Dr David Lewis.

It is dangerous to generalize about any group of people, in particular young people, but surveys, questionnaires, and above all being with and listening to young people are valuable ways to discover the influences and trends affecting them and the beliefs and values they hold.

Understanding the *cultural* trends that affect eleven to fourteens is important, but just as vital is an understanding of the ways they are developing *physically, intellectually, emotionally, socially* and *spiritually*. This combined wealth of knowledge should then be used to influence the style and content of our discipleship programmes.

Big business invests huge amounts of money each year in a wide range of work which examines, analyses and deciphers the world of the young teens. This is not an act of altruism on their part. In 1994 a twelve-year-old averaged a weekly income of £5.30 made up of £3.55 pocket money and £1.75 earned. At fourteen the average income rose to £8.60 with pocket money rising slightly to £4.45 and earnings well up at £3.95.[5] An article in a leading British marketing magazine estimated that the spending potential in 1994 of the seven to fifteen age band was £1bn! With that amount of money around it is little wonder that big business commissions surveys and reports so that they can target children and teens with their materialistic adverts designed to create a need and then meet it with their products.

Christians too can and should access the range of surveys, government statistics and advertising agency reports which are generally available. From them and from information gleaned locally about specific subcultures, it will be possible to gain an insight into the daily lives of young people. For example, national statistics show that one in four thirteen- to fifteen-year-olds are worried about being bullied.[6] Such a high incidence of bullying at school means that both victims and perpetrators will most likely be in a church youth group. Appropriate strategies then must be in place there to ensure that bullying is dealt with and prevented.

National and local surveys can also help us decide what times and day(s) we should meet with those youngsters we are discipling/ nurturing in the faith. Discovering the number who work in legal and illegal part-time or weekend jobs is an important factor.

We need to be creative and flexible about when we ask young people to meet. All too often the time and place for these groups is decided either by tradition or is fixed at the convenience of the group coordinator, which is entirely the wrong way round.

Young people may be taller and have fewer fillings in their teeth than a generation ago, but there are still some worrying trends affecting health. Smoking although decreasing is still prevalent. By the age of fourteen, 15 per cent are already regular smokers with a further 10 per cent occasional smokers.[7] By the age of twelve, 4 per cent drink alcohol at least once a week and a further 10 per cent once or twice a month, with these figures rising to 18 per cent and 25 per cent respectively by the age of fourteen.[8]

According to 1992 Home Office figures, only 3 per cent of twelve- to thirteen-year-olds had taken any kind of illegal drug. However, more recent research suggests that drug abuse is becoming a more widespread problem among this age band. It shows notable levels of

solvent abuse (glue, aerosols, butane gas etc) with around 1 per cent
of twelve- to thirteen-year-olds and 3 per cent of fourteen- to fifteen-
year-olds involved.[9] However, the Central Statistical Office's report
'Special Focus on Children' admit; 'these findings may be conserva-
tive'. Even if they do not experiment with glue, lager or cannabis,
there are plenty of other physical, intellectual, social and emotional
changes taking place to make eleven to fourteens unpredictable. They
live in a peculiar limbo world where they are neither fully children or
fully adults. Often they will demand to be treated like adults, but at
other times they enjoy childrens activities or play.

*Physically* their bodies are changing fast as hormones produce
an increased sexual awareness and the famous 'growth spurt'.
Emerging sexuality reveals itself to the individual by the growth of
the sexual organs and pubic hair. It is also publicly proclaimed as
the boy's voice breaks and the girl's breasts grow. This process can
be alarming and stressful for both sexes. The arms suddenly grow
long while pimples erupt over their unsuspecting faces. And as the
hormones continue their rampage, often masturbation begins with
accompanying guilt and confusion.

Being the first or the last in a similar age group to grow breasts or
start having periods in the case of girls, or grow facial/pubic hair
and have their voice break in boys, is often a nightmare experience.

Issues related to self-image, sex and sexuality will need to be sensitively addressed soon after any initial basics course in Christianity
for new believers. While for churched eleven to fourteens issues like
masturbation and dating, often put off by Christian youth leaders
until they are older, need to be addressed within the context of a
Christian discipleship curriculum.

The 'growth spurt' experienced by this age group also reveals
itself publicly in other ways:

• an increased appetite;

- bursts of energy followed by fatigue;
- longer limbs lead to a lack of coordination and to feelings of awkwardness and lack of self-confidence.

Try to ensure your programme avoids embarrassing the youngsters. A game may sound great in a book, but will it show someone up, or isolate the less athletic? If so, drop or adapt the activity. Losing face is something this age find hard to cope with.

*Intellectually* young people are changing too. Jean Piaget, the Swiss psychologist and one of the pioneers in the field of child development considered that children grow intellectually in a series of spurts which are followed by a calm period of knowledge integration. One of these major changes Piaget identifies as the switch from 'concrete' to 'formal' operations.

According to Piaget, between approximately age six to eleven, a child has the ability to use mental logic based on concrete, real and observable situations. They see issues in terms of right and wrong, black and white – there is no grey area. They mostly accept information as 'fact' and do not question its validity.

However, from about eleven years the ability to make sense of abstract concepts can develop. Some, but not all, begin to work through hypothetical problems and struggle with contradictions. American adolescent psychologist David Elkind calls this new dimension 'thinking in a new key'.

Psychologists Lawrence Kohlberg and James Fowler have also written extensively on moral development and are worth study. Fowler in particular has some interesting theories on faith development, but he should not be read with an uncritical mind.

This new ability to think – to examine themselves and their world abstractly – is a shift which some people never make. Instead they continue to think in concrete terms. This has important implications – Christian theological concepts like sin, salvation and grace are usually taught in a style requiring the ability to think in the abstract. The reason children and young people/adults who think in concrete terms find the sermon at church boring may be because the preacher is talking in abstract terms. On the other hand it may be because the sermon is just plain boring!

It's important to gauge where people are in their learning development. Read a down-market tabloid and compare the way it reports the same event with an up-market broadsheet newspaper and you will discover the difference between communicating to someone who thinks in concrete terms and one who can think abstractly.

As young people develop into this new way of thinking they begin to question everything they formerly accepted unquestioningly. This new ability to think in totally different ways can be very frightening if they see the world as a lonely or dangerous place. They begin to question the actions and policies of the adult generation, leading them into a period of idealism which may not find its full expression until their later teens. They may become vegetarian, join Compassion In World Farming or Greenpeace, but at the same time may be tempted by a burger or prefer to use Dad's petrol guzzling 'taxi service' to riding their eco-friendly pushbike!

Their main preoccupation is thinking about themselves and their situation. They're constantly playing to an imaginary audience, are self-conscious, passionately desire privacy, and spend much of their time in front of the mirror checking their appearance and rehearsing conversations with friends. They often conclude they're not as good-looking, strong or intelligent as others or as they'd like to be. That can lead to feelings of inferiority and worthlessness.

*Emotionally* they can be on a roller-coaster ride of intensity or lethargy. Sometimes they will withdraw and become solitary. Boys in particular can lock into a cycle of simulation or computer games which result in a monk-like existence in their bedroom, only coming out for school, the bathroom or a foray into the kitchen! Others become outgoing and hyperactive. Most ride the high and low tides of intense activity and socializing followed by wallowing in self-pity in isolation.

The emotional task of this age group is shifting as the old support systems change. Increasing independence and a quest for identity (trying to discover where they fit in to this new adult world they are beginning to enter), result in stress and turmoil.

*Socially*, changes partly arising from the emotional changes result in new behaviour patterns which parents in particular can find exhausting and baffling!

Making new discoveries often results in emotional intensity as new feelings and experiences occur. Falling in and out of love can be particularly traumatic and can lead to depression or even a suicide attempt.

Failing to establish friendships with the same or the opposite sex can result in extreme emotions and behaviour.

The youth worker needs to be aware and on the lookout for signs of eating disorders (which can affect boys as well as girls), depression or other emotional peaks and troughs.

The intensity of their emotions means this age band are particularly susceptible to emotional appeals. Care and integrity are required of all who work with young people. In evangelistic meetings and other situations where manipulative strategies can result in a purely emotional response from young people, particular care is required.

Explosive and fiery outbursts of anger from normally placid youngsters are another common manifestation of the emotional cauldron bubbling away under the surface. I'm not suggesting that a wild temper should be lightly excused, but understanding that this is quite common may make the unsuspecting youth worker a little more prepared!

Other behavioural changes as a result of this search for identity involve:

- Experimentation – they try out new behaviour patterns, testing and bending the previously accepted word of parent(s) and other authority figures, adopting the potential identities of role-models – friends, a celebrity, an adult friend they respect etc.

- Belonging – it is essential for the young adolescent to feel they 'belong' to a peer group. They frequently adopt a special style of clothes (or wear them in a particular way). A new 'in' language appears. Habits, values and opinions have to be accepted.

- Acceptance by the opposite sex – this in itself leads to the changing of habits and behaviour.

- Being different from adults – a clear line of demarcation has to be established between youngsters and surrounding adults, helping to create a special culture for the youngsters.

The search for identity can make this age group insecure. They knew how to be a child – how can they cope with being an adult? As part of this quest for identity, there's a desire for independence from what they often consider to be 'oppressive' parents. Such an abrupt independence is neither practical nor financially possible but the youngster starts by shifting his emotional reliance from parents to friends of a similar age. The rise of friendship over and (sometimes) against 'the family' usually comes first with youngsters of the same sex before going on to include members of the opposite sex.

These factors lead to a dilemma for youth leaders/workers. The constant shifting of emotions and the whirlwind of social changes make it difficult to predict what mood the kids are going to be in and how they feel towards each other.

There are times when the boys and girls need to talk separately. Single-sex nurture groups have proved successful in many situations. Yet without members of the opposite sex being around, some kids may see little point in being there!

The key is to be as real and constant as possible and so become good role models for the youngsters. Youth workers are often the adults closest to youngsters who are more likely to confide in them than in their parents.

That is what incarnational ministry is all about. Just as Jesus spent time with people to show them what God is really like, so we need to spend time with young people – modelling Christ to them. This has big implications for the youth worker who can become a pseudo-parent and great care should be exercised not to add to an already potentially tense relationship between youthworker and the youngsters' parent(s).

When an eleven- to fourteen-year-old from an unchurched background becomes a believer, the relationship between the church and the parent(s) needs to be treated with great care. Any responsible parents are likely to be concerned and view this new 'faith' as potentially dangerous. Their minds will be full of fears and questions such as:

- Has my son/daughter joined a mind-bending cult?

- Will they start preaching at me over breakfast?

- Will the time they spend on church activities harm their school studies?

- Will the values and life goals they have nurtured in their children be snatched away and replaced?

- Who are these people their son/daughter quotes so authoritatively?

It is important that the youth leader and/or minister request a meeting with the parent(s) to explain that they are not creatures from the black lagoon who want to corrupt their child! Sometimes a 'clearing the air', one-off meeting is enough, but it is advisable to write or phone occasionally to ask if they have any questions or problems about their child's church links that they want to talk

through. In the majority of cases this attitude of openness is enough
to ensure that the parent(s) are satisfied and prepared to allow their
Billy or Susie to attend church/youth group.

We must encourage the eleven- to fourteen-year-old new convert
to witness sensitively to their family members. All too often a zealous
young new Christian has launched into a 'You're going to hell and
you need to repent of gambling and getting drunk' diatribe, which is
more likely to make parents angry than bring them to the cross!

Encourage any young firebrands in your discipleship group to
demonstrate by their lifestyle the change that has taken place in
their life. A clean bedroom, getting home in time for meals and
offering to wash up are more likely to be a good witness than a
sermon about a need for salvation.

*Spiritually,* the early teen years are a critical time in the development of young people. As youngsters shift from the concrete to the
abstract, so the old interpretations of Christian teaching are
reassessed and may be jettisoned for a more mature way of
thinking. Before a person can learn that God is Spirit and Truth,
he/she has to unlearn the acquired notion that God is an old man
with a beard sitting on a cloud.

Initially pre-teens who grow up in the church may conform to
what they think are the expectations of their parents or other
authority figures, including church leaders. They'll often respond to
questions with what they think are the 'right' answers rather than
the truthful ones. This surface acceptance of the orthodox often
covers an inner crisis as they reassess what is true to them personally. At the same time, even if they're able to make those belief
adjustments they may also feel that appearing 'religious' to their
peers would destroy their street cred and alienate them from their
primary source of belonging.

The key task of Christian nurturing is to help the eleven- to fourteen-year-old to decide clearly the answer to two questions:

- What is true for me personally?
- What do I believe to be the truth about God and everything that goes with it?

Unless we're able to help them develop a mature way of thinking about God, they'll simply put God in the same category as Father Christmas or the Tooth Fairy!

---

**EXERCISE**

Work through the list below and try to come up with a concrete illustration, example or dramatic way of communicating these abstract theological concepts which are central to an under-standing of the gospel of Christ, so that an unchurched youth who has not yet developed the ability to think in abstract terms can understand and relate to these theological concepts.

REPENTANCE    FORGIVENESS    SIN    GRACE

JUDGMENT    SALVATION    FAITH    ATONEMENT

---

1  BMRB Youth TGI 1993
2  Ibid
3  Ibid
4  TSB Lifestyle survey by pollsters Taylor Newton 1993
5  Ibid
6  Teenage Religion and Values by Leslie J. Francis and William K. Kay (Gracewing) 1995
7  Office of Population Census and Surveys, 1992
8  Ibid
9  Home Office 1992

# The World of the Fifteen- to Eighteen-Year-Old

'Suddenly everything got very serious – it was quite a shock,' says fifteen-year-old Andrew on entering what could be his final two years of education. The increased pressure from parents and teachers to work hard and achieve good GCSE grades, plus the realization that without good results he will struggle to find any sort of job, let alone a good one, mean that Andrew like others of his age faces new stresses.

In many GCSE subjects, course work is assessed and these marks contribute to the overall grade. So the fifteen- and sixteen-year-old needs to perform consistently well and then put in an extra spurt of revision to prepare for the dreaded exams.

Andrew also does a paper round but is hoping to get a Saturday job in a supermarket which will pay much better. 'Ten pounds a week, is hard to live on,' says Andrew.

He spends most of his free time with his two best mates and their wider circle of friends. About once a month he gets drunk at a party but has so far managed to escape detection by his parents who rightly see him as fairly reliable and responsible.

Chloe his seventeen-year-old sister works at a hairdresser's. Unlike most YTS trainees she was kept on at the end of her two years of training, or as Chloe describes it, 'slave labour'.

Unlike the majority of her class who chose to stay at school to take A-Levels or retake GCSEs, Chloe decided to leave and try to get a job. Her three grade 'C' GCSEs didn't seem to help much, and after much arm-twisting from her parents she took up the YTS option.

Now Chloe regrets her decision to leave school. She looks with envy at Rachel, Samantha and Kerry, three of her classmates who are about to enter university.

'If I could go back in time I would have stayed on to try and get good enough qualifications for university and then taken a year out to travel abroad.'

Chloe can only afford to go to the pub with her friends two nights a week, and even then she has to watch how many drinks she buys. 'The barman knows I'm underage but I don't have much problem getting served. One day I'd like to start up my own hairdressing business, but I can't see that happening for a long while, because I would need to save a lot of money and persuade a bank manager to let me borrow money. They won't take a risk like that with me at my age, will they?'

The decisions that fifteen- to eighteen-year-olds make about educational and vocational training are critical enough. But this age group also makes decisions about where they see themselves fitting into society (or not) which are even more vital to their future destiny. The decisions they make during their mid-to-late teens will for the majority shape their future life goals, their political and religious views and their socio-economic standing.

One of the reasons why Christian youthwork is so important and so rewarding is because, for the majority of people, it's now or never regarding the claims of Christ. Ask any group of Christian adults when they made the decision to become a disciple of Jesus Christ and the majority will say it was in their teenage years. And even those who grew into faith from their childhood, the teenage years, particularly when they left school for employment, higher education or the dole, will say that the mid-to-late teens was a time of crucial re-examination and testing of their faith.

The make-or-break experience of deciding whether they will stand up and be counted as believers away from the safe environment of home and church is critical. That is why we need to understand and respond appropriately to the various *cultural, physical, intellectual, emotional, social* and *spiritual* pressures and changes affecting the mid-to-late teens.

Some *cultural* trends appear to be global. With the world-wide access to MTV on cable or satellite young people in Bangkok, Beirut, Berlin and Birmingham can be watching the same advert promoting the same product. One commentator has called this phenomenon the attempted Coca-Colonization of the world! Some music, jeans, footwear and soft drinks have achieved global penetration into the world of the fifteen- to eighteen-year-old. Other important trends are restricted to national boundaries, while many more subcultures exist in each city, town and neighbourhood.

Advertising agencies have discovered that this age group is amongst the most technologically and culturally aware group in society. A *naive* attempt by them to advertise their product to this group of media-drenched people will surely backfire. Many advertisers employ people full-time to research this age group, recognizing that it takes a sophisticated and clever approach to win them over to their message.

During the early 1990s ad agencies have been telling companies about rave. At the time of writing this remains the dominant movement in British youth culture. On a typical weekend huge numbers of young people attend a rave or dance club. Over a third of teenagers have attended a rave. But unlike so many other youth trends, rave culture has grown organically. It developed despite, rather than because of large record companies, radio stations or media gurus.

The movement began in a handful of clubs in Manchester and London in 1987. Within a few years it had mushroomed into a large number of illegal warehouse parties and outdoor raves which routinely attracted tens of thousands. By early 1995 rave music dominated the pop charts.

Most musical genres have a spiritual undercurrent: they have a message as well as a medium and rave is no different. Reggae has strong links with Rastafarianism, Soul has its roots in Black gospel music, big names in mainstream rock such as Peter Gabriel and Tina Turner have links with Eastern religions, many Heavy Metal bands have adopted occult images, while Punk was nihilistic.

Within rave culture there is a definite but confused connection with hedonistic paganism and Eastern philosophy that make up the teachings we call New Age. Some bands such as The Shamen are explicit promoters of this spirituality, while others are more implicit and suggestive. Rave is irreverent with a wilful sense of humour. Ravers want a good time and they want it now. In the frantic atmosphere of a rave charged with loud back-to-back dance music and cheap Ecstasy, a kind of chemical fellowship is created as people sweatily bop the night away.

The connection between pop culture and recreational drugs is not new, but the cheapness and relative availability of Ecstasy, which is an amphetamine with an added hallucinogenic effect, means that tens if not hundreds of thousands of British teenagers have taken 'E'.

However, although the drug link with rave is well-documented and undeniable, it would be a wild miscalculation to say that all ravers take drugs. But even if a fifteen to eighteen-year-old does not attend raves or dance clubs, it would be foolish to presume they are not being touched and influenced by the messages, spirituality and values of the rave scene.

Companies like Britvic, Coca Cola, Golden Wonder and Sega have invested heavily in information on rave culture. They discovered that the rave music scene is characterized by its functionality – there are no stars, no megagroups and no obsessive knowledge about every detail of a favourite band. Ravers are not into rebellion so much as cynicism. They also noted the sociability, fellowship and warmth created at raves.

With the fifteen- to twenty-four age band in the UK enjoying a spending potential of £½bn,[1] big business used their hard-won information on rave culture to create clever crafted messages to appeal to them. The results were ads like Sega Pirate TV, Golden Wonder pots and the brilliantly successful Tango ads of 1994. Britvic, who manufacture the Tango brand enjoyed commercial success in 1994/5 with their award-winning zany adverts, perfectly matched the raw humour of this age band at the time.

We can learn from what these companies discovered and should listen carefully to their researchers. Men like Charlie Sampson, board account director for ad agency Cowan Kemsley Taylor who says: 'Rave culture's emphasis on accessibility and participation has led young people to reject icons, hype and aspirational, image-based or passive advertising. They are interested in experience, not image. They respond to advertising that involves them in some way, not something that just says, "Look at me".'

If secular companies are interested to discover youth culture so that they can sell into it, how much more should we, messengers and guardians of the good news, be keen to know youth culture?

The New Testament makes it clear that the Apostle Paul was adept at learning from and adapting local culture with the gospel message to aid his communication to widely differing audiences. Compare Paul's communication methods described in Acts 13:13–41 where he spoke to a group of Jews in the synagogue in Antioch in Pisidia, alongside Acts 17:16–34 where he addresses Gentile Athenians.

To the Jews he gives an Old Testament history lesson which links the Messiah figure with the person of Jesus. His Jewish audience would have appreciated Paul's knowledge of their heritage even if the final conclusion would have left them uncomfortable or even angry.

To the Athenians Paul quotes two of their local poets; Epimendides and Aratus to support part of his argument and also refers to a local landmark, the altar to the unknown god in the city. Paul skilfully uses local culture to his advantage. By taking time and effort and by study and then using this information wisely he is able to communicate effectively to vastly different audiences. A Jewish history lesson to these Athenians would have left them snoringly bored! Instead they have regular local references to keep them listening. To use Paul's own words, he 'became all things to all men to save them by whatever means possible.'

You and I need to do the same. If we don't know about rave culture, about the New Age and hedonism which philosophically drive rave culture, our communication to young people who relate to rave culture will be more likely to miss the mark. Instead of communication we'll be spreading confusion, like the newly converted woman from the East End of London who was given an Authorized Version of the Bible was confused and indeed horrified to read St Paul's advice that she should 'put to death the old man'! While remaining true to the essential heart of the gospel we must constantly re-enculturate it so that we avoid unnecessarily making the message remote from non-believers.

But if we fully identify with young people, ministering to them with an incarnational model will create potential problems between us and the church. By becoming a bridge between church and unchurched youth culture you risk misunderstanding by other Christians who often identify culturally sensitive evangelism as liberalism. Since the 1970s some evangelical Christian leaders were openly critical and hostile to others who formed Christian rock bands. Rock was attacked as 'the devils music' and any Christians who used this method to communicate were beyond the pale. A book was published and widely quoted which attacked this attempt to enculturate the gospel. Similarly, in the 1990s Christians who have adopted rave/dance music and successfully communicate a positive message through that medium have also been criticized.

This phenomenon is not new. The great pioneering missionary to

China, Hudson Taylor, chose to wear the clothes and even the pigtail of the Chinese peasants he sought to win for Christ. Other Western missionaries derided him for adopting the local culture. While they built Gothic-style church buildings and dressed in suits, Hudson Taylor, adopting St Paul's methods, cared more about saving souls than wearing stiff collars. History records that Hudson Taylor saw more fruit from his labours than all his critics put together.

Jesus was a poor man. From a disreputable town, he worked as a carpenter, lived among the working classes, ate what they ate, wore what they wore. The common people, the working class and the underclass easily identified with him. But Christ's understanding, wisdom and love for people meant that *all* classes and people could readily identify with him.

Sadly many young people today regard church as a club for the middle classes, and sadly, in some locations, they are right! But understanding the world of fifteen- to eighteen-year-olds is not restricted to an understanding of their culture. It requires knowledge of and a response to other changes and influences which affect them.

The *intellectual* developments that continue to take place as young people move through their teenage years is another important factor to take account of when seeking effectively to minister to them.

One big difference between this age band and most adults is their relationship with technology. This is the first generation to feel at home with computers. Intellectually they are tuned in to using new technologies. Almost to a man (and woman) they love computers. Their manual dexterity around a keyboard leaves older people feeling awkward and stumbling. From their first years in education, computers played a part in their learning.

'The trouble is that modern man has transferred his worship of

God to a worship of technology.'[2] The words that this age group read from a computer screen are given more weight and authority than the human voice. This is a fast-changing situation and further technological advances in the next few years are likely to result in new opportunities and new potential dangers. Two changes that are imminent are the advent of easy access into what has been called the Information Superhighway (Internet) and cheaper interactive entertainment centre CD-Rom computers and their software.

Christian youth workers are among the first Christians to experiment in these areas. Increasing numbers are making contact on the Internet and are using the new technologies to spice up their youth programming.

It is also important to understand and respond to changes in the teaching methods within education. Many of us will have been taught in a very different style from teenagers today. When I asked a teacher to tell me how he taught, he wrote the following statement:

> Young people and children are taught and learn in a variety of situations using a range of methods. Through experimenting, hypothesising, investigating, drama, problem solving, story, discussion etc, they develop their skills, attitudes, knowledge and conceptual understanding. Very few lessons are based on the old method of 'chalk and talk'. Through structured programmes which involve repetition, consolidation and developing of concepts, children are able to increase their knowledge and understanding of the task in hand.

Compare the range of teaching methods listed above which are typically employed in schools today with the range of teaching methods used in a church service, a youth fellowship or in a nurture group. Chances are that the variety of teaching methods in a school will vastly outnumber the church/youth fellowship/nurture group.

By the time young people leave school at sixteen or eighteen they will have grown used to learning through a variety of stimuli, far beyond mere chalk-and-talk style teaching. The days when a teacher would stand in front of his class and give a lecture-style talk for forty-five minutes and then set a list of questions to test comprehension are long dead. But the problem is that in too many churches and church-based youth groups there is a false expectation that this style of communication and teaching is sufficient.

Some even go further by suggesting that a thirty-minute long sermon is a biblical model of Christian teaching and that interactive learning, role play, experimentation, use of drama and audio visuals, etc, are at best trendy, at worst unchristian. I believe the lecture-based sermon has a place within the overall nurture and care of young people, but it is just one element within a wide range of communication and teaching tools which should be used. Certainly, Jesus preached. But that wasn't the only method of communication he used. In fact, apart from the Sermon on the Mount recorded in Matthew's Gospel, Jesus' 'sermons' if they can be called that, were short and punchy and were outnumbered by other teaching methods.

Intellectually this generation of fifteens to eighteens have had significantly different educational and intellectual shaping from older generations. Our programming must take account of this.

*Emotionally* this age group is still growing towards maturity. An eighteen-year-old may look mature, well-balanced and fully developed, but in his/her emotional life is still growing and changing. Many will have lost their virginity and for some of the girls this will not have been a positive experience. Guilt, deceit, rejection, betrayal, loss and bitterness are just some of the negative emotions which can surface as a result of sexual liaisons. Their bodies may be mature but the ability to respond in a mature way to the new possibilities which independence brings may be lacking.

One of the most important skills which youth workers need to develop in order to respond appropriately to emotional hurts is *listening*. It's a corny saying, but it is true; 'God gave us one mouth and two ears, so why don't we talk less and listen more?' I believe that many mid-to-late teens long for an adult who will listen to them. Often it is their main complaint about parents; 'They don't listen to me!' Listening to young people aids learning. You will learn about particular and general problems, pressures, influences, attitudes, value systems and a whole lot else if you actually stop and listen.

I met a youth leader from Wales who told me about her church open youth club. It was called The Lighthouse. Like many poorly run open youth clubs the leaders merely acted as wardens. They saw their role as protecting the building and its equipment from misuse and damage. Their relationship with the youngsters was distant and mainly restricted to authoritarian confrontations. It took them eighteen months to discover the kids called the club the 'Sad House', a discovery made only when one of the workers began talking and listening to the young people. The leaders just didn't listen.

Even when we do listen, it is often not effective listening. Instead we are thinking about what we are going to say in reply instead of giving them 100 per cent of our attention. Young people are used to adults who fail to pay attention and really listen to them. If we really listen to them the comparison will be striking. We will then begin to hear the feeling and true meaning behind what they say. We will *really hear* them.

I adopt a method called 'Listening and reflecting' to help me listen effectively, because I am naturally not a good listener. This technique is widely used in counselling situations and it works very well. Like most effective techniques it is extremely simple.

As you listen to the youngster, every so often simply recap on what they have said. E.g. 'So what you are saying is that your friend

Sam doesn't understand that you need time on your own every now and then. . .' This occasional précis-style recap ensures that you have heard correctly and gives the young person the chance to correct you if you have misheard or misunderstood. It will ensure that we hear what they tell us instead of what we think they are saying! This is important because we all have preconceived ideas of what people mean when we hear something we *think* we can relate to. Instead of continuing actively to listen, we race ahead to a conclusion and a response. It is vital that we do not assume what a young person is going to say. Beware of making premature assumptions.

Also try to avoid saying; 'I know exactly how you feel.' The chances are that you don't! One twenty-something male youth leader told me of an occasion when a girl told him that her period meant her emotions were all over the place. Before he could stop himself he heard himself say to her; 'I know exactly how you feel!'

As we get better at listening, we will begin to listen not just to people's words but also their body language and their silences which can also tell us a lot.

The result of all this listening should lead to 'empathy'. Paul tells us to; 'Be happy with those who are happy, weep with those that weep' (Romans 12:15). Crying with a person who is crying calls for a greater emotion than mere sympathy; it requires empathy.

The dictionary definition of empathy is; imaginatively experiencing another person's experiences, appreciating the feeling of something fully.

When Jesus wept at Lazarus's tomb he was aware that within moments he could summon Lazarus from his grave, but because he cared for Mary and Martha, and empathized with their feelings of deep grief, he cried – he felt their pain.

Accurate listening will help us empathize with others and share their highs and lows – and to be sure young people will have plenty of emotional high and low points!

Not surprisingly experts in adolescent development have differing theories. However, certain names like Piaget, mentioned in the previous chapter stand out as recognized sources of insight and wisdom.

As we consider the *moral* and *spiritual* development of young people it is important to consider the findings and opinions of others who have built on the work of Piaget and developed his theories.

Erikson characterizes the mid-to-late teens as a period when the young person decides either on the intimacy of close relationships, which may include marriage, or a life of isolation due to fear of intimacy.

Erikson was also among the first to describe the self-doubt and questioning that adolescents experience as they develop their own values, morality and beliefs. It is a period of doubt, questioning and search for identity.

Another to build on Piaget's theories, Kohlberg, developed widely held views on moral development. He identified various stages that children and adolescents pass through, although some do not reach maturity and develop to the fullest stages.

Kohlberg identified five stages:

1 *Punishment* where moral behaviour is influenced by a child's reasoning on whether a course of action will result in disapproval and punishment.

2 *Reciprocity* marks the next phase where a belief that fairness and equality are the bases for relationships and, according to Kohlberg, can develop from the age of seven.

3 *Good girl – good boy* is the stage where the approval and favour of others is the deciding factor.

4 *Law and order* consists of a sense of duty, where maintaining the
  social order is a governing factor. Kohlberg believes this fourth stage
  is often attained during teenage years.

Kohlberg believes that some individuals transcend the fourth stage
to make moral decisions on the basis of principles rather than what
he calls 'conventional thinking' (stages 1 to 4). Kohlberg's theories
consist more of structure than content, something which has caused
Christians to criticize his work.

The final 'big name' in moral development to take note of, James
Fowler, builds on the work of Piaget, Erikson and Kohlberg. He has
identified various 'faith' stages in the child and adolescent which
deserve more study than this chapter allows. *Stages of Faith* by
James Fowler (Harper and Row, San Francisco 1981) is a landmark
book.

Fowler describes the key faith-deciding years of adolescence as
the 'individuative-reflective' stage, when beliefs are analysed and
critically questioned.

The problem with these theories is that they tend to be built on a
view which ignores the power of God to change people and His
sovereign right to work according to his own agenda and not a pre-
directed agenda from humankind. Piaget and the others have some
useful ideas worth considering, but God will be God!

One other point worth considering about the spiritual development of this age group is the prevailing trend towards 'feelings'.
Many young people are becoming addicted to experiences which
feel good or exciting. From a young age many have been fed an
adrenaline-driven diet of thrills from a variety of sources, including TV, ever more realistic computer games and white-knuckle
theme-park rides, which in adolescence results in a low-boredom
threshold. Fast-paced variety could be said to be their watchword,
and this has implications for their spiritual growth.

Many teenage Christians (and adults too!) place a high degree of importance on 'feeling good' about their Christian faith. Not necessarily a bad thing, of course, but this expectation that church services will be fun, fast-paced, culturally relevant and provide lots of personally satisfying experiences is often not matched by the reality on offer.

*The English Church Census* of 1989 showed that the Charismatic House Church/New Church stream had a higher percentage of young people in their congregations than any other Protestant denomination. More relevant and modern worship is one factor, a friendliness and flexible attitude by adult church members towards the youngsters is possibly another.

But the emphasis on the work of the Holy Spirit and an expectation that God wants to touch and affect our emotions as well as our intellect is surely a key contributory factor to the relative success the New Churches have had among this generation of young people. The more recent phenomenon known as 'The Toronto Blessing' may satisfy this hunger to 'feel' God yet further. Certainly any nurture and discipling of young people which backs away from facilitating young people to experience the power of God personally will not only be poorer spiritually but is also likely to be less attractive to the 'experience-seeking' teen of today.

However, a balance must be struck here. In the past, an emphasis on factual, logical accumulation of Bible knowledge left the disciple dry. But an overemphasis on experience and feelings to the detriment of providing the doctrinal foundations will result in 'feel-good' junkies who don't really know what they believe, but merely seek the next non-chemical high.

Knowledge and experience together is what is required to facilitate spiritual development.

The *social development* of a fifteen- to eighteen-year-old is one of the most outwardly obvious changes taking place in his/her life.

Increasing independence from parental control and influence occurs simultaneously with an increase in influence from peers over behaviour patterns, opinions, ambitions and lifestyle. The influence that adolescents have over each other is profound and has far-reaching effects. Commonly called 'peer pressure', many parents consider this to be always a negative and destructive force.

Peer pressure within a Christian youth fellowship or nurture group can be a positive force. When a young person wavers in his/her faith, the encouragement and positive example of a peer can make the difference between the youngster dropping out and losing faith or hanging in there.

However, small youth groups should make sure their programme includes opportunities for the group to mix with other larger groups of Christian young people to help avoid the minority ghetto complex that commonly exists.

All too often teenage Christians consider they are somehow 'odd' by being Christian. The benefit of feeling part of a large group of peers who all share the same faith and lifestyle values is enormous and helps dispel the myth of oddness. Being part of a large dynamic group of one's peers who are worshipping God, serving God and telling others about God can be a very exciting, uplifting feeling. It tells the young person 'you belong with us' and 'we are a strong and vibrant group worth being part of.'

Church growth experts suggest that adult believers flourish best when provided with meetings with other Christians in three dimensions – small 'cell' groups of between four and ten, medium-size 'communities' where they can know everyone which number between fifty and two hundred, and large-scale town-wide 'celebrations' where five hundred to two thousand meet together to celebrate Christ and the oneness they share.

If this is helpful for adults, how much more crucial is it for mid-to-late teens for whom social contact and peer bonding is so important.

Christian youth leaders and churches must stop focusing on the negative aspects of peer pressure and start exploiting their positive faith-building capacities. The wise youth worker uses peer pressure to work for him/her and also teaches and equips young people to deal with the negative power it can exert.

Many young people are ignorant of how they can be influenced by peer pressure. Practical teaching on how to stand up assertively for their beliefs will help prevent them being sucked into destructive behaviour or habits.

It should also be recognized that young people naturally form groups based on common interests and backgrounds. Too often churches have attempted to incorporate new youngsters within an existing youth group without reference to whether they will mix well.

Middle-class Christians who have grown up within the church will find a new influx of unchurched working/underclass young people hard to relate to. Often one group will prevail while the others diminish and leave, feeling this isn't their scene.

A better tactic would have been to recognize their differentness and to set up a separate meeting for the newer group. Occasional socials or other meetings where both groups attend could be arranged to help begin the mixing process while still running the groups as separate entities. In time the two groups may merge, but often their needs will be so different that this is inappropriate.

Too often the needs of the leaders and lack of staffing have resulted in artificial groups which do not gel and result in the alienation and resentment of one or both sets of kids.

Awareness of the social groupings of young people in and outside your church is an important part of your education. Some social group identities will be obvious by their 'uniform' of clothes and hairstyle. But others will be outwardly more subtle in their differences, but when you listen to their values, interests and aspirations it becomes apparent that they are different from others. One of the best places to identify these different groups is in school and college.

Many churches recognize the need to provide different services and meetings for the different parts of the local adult community; we need to appreciate that the more socially aware teenager's needs are valid too. I am not suggesting that Paul's statement in Galatians 3:28 that in Christ there is neither Jew nor Greek, male nor female etc, is invalid. Far from it, I believe we need to encourage all-age, all-social groups meeting together to share, worship and learn. But I also believe that our differentness and our different needs should not be ignored. In churches which stress the 'all-one-in-Christ' argument as to why they do not provide different meetings for different social groups, I believe it is often just a convenient excuse to avoid the undoubted extra effort required to provide variety. The result of a monotone church is that it predominantly reaches just one social grouping and age band. A few hardy souls may survive who are different from the rest, but that is despite, not because of the monosystem.

This is not the place to enter into the youth church argument, except to say that since many churches are 'senior citizens churches', or 'middle-aged-with-grown-up-children churches', (not in name maybe, but look around the congregation and that is the reality), why not 'youth churches'!

Another important development in the social aspect of the fifteen- to nineteen-year-old is dating, sexual relationships and the peculiarly sexist attitude that a young man who has had several sexual liaisons is a 'stud', while a young woman with similar sexual experience is likely to be branded a 'slut'.

I believe we need to teach biblical principles about relationships and sex regularly to this age group. They already get information about masturbation, heavy petting, homosexuality, abortion, breaking up, premarital sex, AIDS and STDs from a variety of other sources which are at best humanistic, at worst pagan and hedonistic.

As well as teaching, it is important to provide opportunities for teenage Christians to meet other teenage Christians of the opposite sex.

If you have a group of sixteen-year-old girls and just one spotty, anorak-clad, train-spotting lad, they are going to look elsewhere! If your youth group doesn't meet up with other Christian youth groups your girls will definitely date non-Christian lads. While that may not be the end of the world, the chances are the sexual morals of the non-Christian lads will not be better than those of Christian lads, rather the reverse.

If we care about the young people in our groups, we need to care about every aspect of their being. Holistic ministry includes facilitating meetings with teenage Christians of the opposite sex to build non-sexual friendships.

*Intellectually* as the adolescent grows from early to mid-and-late teens the period of questioning, which can be very difficult for both teen and parent, continues. Often it leads to experimentation with different lifestyles, political, moral and ethical standpoints, as they struggle to discover their own identity. This is no bad thing.

Questioning the basic foundations on which they are going to build their lives can be a worrying time for Christian parents as they see their model son or daughter experiment with being an eco-aware hippy or a militant Marxist. But in this process many young people find or rediscover faith for themselves. This faith is actually a much stronger one than the borrowed values and set of beliefs handed down to them by their parents because it is truly their own and so is not usually a carbon copy of their parents' faith.

Their radical stance on discipleship may threaten the more comfortable and respectable style of Christianity of an older generation. The young may find the forms of worship of their parents' church too staid and boring and seek a more expressive and liberated setting to worship. But the parents, the church, and the young people need to encourage and seek to understand each other rather than feel threatened and defensive. Sometimes this new radicalism of their children can actually breathe new life and vitality into the stale faith of parents. It can be a breath of fresh air!

By comparison, young people who are pressured by parents or others into conforming to certain standards and styles are most likely to rebel in a dramatic and potentially damaging way. It is no coincidence that the teenage children of pastors and vicars are often those who rebel against Christianity most fiercely. In attempting to portray a picture of family unity to their parish/congregation, ministers sow the seeds of resentment which will eventually result in a bitter harvest.

Even those who choose not to reject publicly the faith of their parents may privately have a paper-thin hold on Christianity. Once they are away from home, at university or in a job surrounded by non-believers, they compromise what little faith they had. Like the seed grown in stony ground their roots were not established or deep. They wither in the heat when the testing time arrive. Allowing for, even encouraging a questioning attitude towards faith and prompting youth to experiment within certain boundaries, are more likely, though not guaranteed, to result in a faith that will endure.

1 *Marketing Week* Magazine 1994
2 *Future Shock*, Alvin Toffler (Random House)

# Discipling Churched Young People

Laura was in my youth group a few years ago. She was painfully shy and hardly ever said a word despite all our efforts to include her in conversations and make her feel wanted. Her parents were fairly new Christians, and despite her silence, she seemed to settle down well in the church. It was a great moment when I baptized her. One of the last events she ever came to was a 'Spiritual Boot Camp' designed to give tough, no-nonsense teaching to kids who really wanted to be heroes for Jesus.

Laura wanders the streets now with a bottle of cider and a new baby. She lives with an odd assortment of drug pushers and 'crusties'. She smells dreadfully and looks worse. Sometimes she drops in to a church service, but she never stays long.

Michael went off with us on an overseas trip where for three weeks he shared his faith with all comers on the streets of a major foreign city. He had always been torn between his Christian upbringing and his desire to be 'one of the lads', but it looked as if he had firmly and finally decided where he stood.

It was only a few weeks after returning home that Michael dropped out. I've seen him several times since. He's full of excuses, very embarrassed but clearly not disposed to return. For the moment, at least, God can take a back seat.

'Discipling' used to be a word we used about new Christians – people who had come into the church from outside. More and more, that isn't the case. Young people brought up in church families are dropping away from their allegiance with alarming frequency. There have always been drop-outs, but now it's a mass exodus. How do we ensure that churched young people – Sunday-school graduates, sons of elders, daughters of the manse – actually stay with us and grow into mature, confident faith?

One thing is certain. They *won't* stay unless we appreciate that there are particular pressures associated with being a churched kid. We can't use the same discipling strategy we employ with young people from other backgrounds. The children of church families have their own advantages – and their own problems too.

## Advantages for Church-Based Youth

There are at least four reasons why it should be easier to disciple churched kids than others.

### 1 Knowledge of the Scriptures
Paul saw this as a real advantage for Timothy (2 Timothy 3:14–16). He didn't have to learn basic Christian concepts from scratch – they were already implanted. We can't take too much for granted, of course; some young people leave our Sunday schools with start-lingly little biblical grasp! But any knowledge of the Bible however defective gives them a head start.

### 2 Supportive environment
New Christians from pagan homes may face total astonishment from their mum and dad; churched kids have (at least theoretically) parents who want them to find faith and an adult church which longs to greet them as members. Of course, this doesn't always happen – the family may be uncaring and the church cold. But the likelihood is that a decision to follow Christ will be easier to pursue in this environment than in any other.

## 3 Regular contact systems

Churched kids are already in contact with people who can help them grow. They know youth workers, church leaders, former Sunday-school teachers, friends of the family, perhaps other Christians of their own age. They may have been to Spring Harvest or other events where many kinds of help are available. For them it isn't a case of entering a strange new culture and meeting lots of unfamiliar people.

## 4 Cultural closeness to a Christian lifestyle

These young people have grown up in an environment where Christian moral ideals are recognized, where Christian standards are practised. To adjust their own lifestyle to a discipleship model doesn't take as much of a radical shift as might otherwise be necessary.

So why do the Lauras and Michaels continue to drop out? It's because being churched creates its own problems too. Timothy started with advantages, but he seems also to have been a little diffident and timid in his approach to life. For fifteen different reasons, an upbringing in the church can be a mixed blessing . . .

# Problems for Church-Based Youth

## 1 Unapplied knowledge

C S Lewis once commented that we all have a tendency to think without acting – in other words, to stuff into our minds bits of information which we never put into practice. And the more we think without acting, he said, 'the less becomes our capacity to act'. Church-based young people have absorbed a lot of scriptural teaching but may never have acted on what they know. They are well aware of what they should do – they just never do it. And the more they know, the less likely they are to do anything about it.

## 2  Cynicism

When young people have knocked about in the average church for a while, they will have witnessed several blatant examples of human sinfulness and hypocrisy. Given the teenage tendency to be idealistic – 'things shouldn't be like this' – and the teenage tendency to write off everything substandard, it's easy to see that this can lead to scathing cynicism.

## 3  Instant spiritual gianthood

Some of the least appealing churched kids are those who preen themselves on their biblical knowledge and spiritual awareness. This can be unwittingly encouraged by proud parents and unwise youth leaders ('Edwin is just fifteen, but he's so mature in the Lord'). Spiritual pride leads to a fall, often via doctrinal fads. Big-headed Christian kids are the ones who embrace eccentric teachings and regret it later.

## 4  Parental *laissez-faire*

Sometimes Christian parents have extremely low levels of expectation of their kids ('Oh, well, boys will be boys . . . we were all like that at their age'). Sometimes it's because they had a fairly strict upbringing themselves and are scared that their teenager will be alienated from the church if they make too many rules. Sometimes it's because the parents are so involved in church life themselves that they simply don't notice the lack of spiritual development in their children's lives.

## 5  The standard set by the youth group

All teenagers follow the crowd. And if their 'crowd' is a Christian youth group in which low standards of Christian living are predominant, they will tend to adopt those standards unthinkingly. They may have little awareness that this is not real Christian living. They may be victims of 'cultural' Christianity, living by certain guidelines because it's the way their friends live, but with little genuine conviction of their own.

## 6  Identification of Jesus with Sunday school
When earliest childhood memories are of flannelgraphs and choruses, it can be difficult to perceive that Christianity is an adult faith. 'Jesus is for the babies.'

## 7  A cotton-wool upbringing
Many churched kids are so successfully cushioned from the harshness of real life by their parents that one of two unfortunate things happens. Either the outside world starts to look more fascinating to them than it really is or else they develop a fear of it and try to retreat inside a 'safe' religious ghetto rather than growing into mature adulthood.

## 8  Adult leaders
Many church leaders look back on their own youth and assume that they know what true commitment in teenagers will look like when they see it. But often their definition is culturally twenty years out of date, and they fail to recognize and appreciate true stirrings of the grace of God in youngsters who don't look like their ideal.

## 9  Lack of good resources
We have lots of good teaching materials for children. We have lots of good study books for adults. We're developing a better range of group materials for adolescents. But there is very little which teenagers can take and use by themselves in order to lay the foundations of personal Bible study on a level they can understand. And unless time with God becomes an individual commitment, the roots of personal relationship with the Lord Jesus may never go very deep.

## 10 Split families

An increasing number of churched kids come from families in which one partner is a Christian and the other isn't. Especially where this split in outlook is compounded by divorce, it can be hard for young people to work out unemotionally and logically what they think and believe about Jesus.

## 11 Previous 'experiences'

Some Christian young people have been encouraged to seek experiences for which they are not ready and the results have bred cynicism. I've seen too many thirteen-year-old burnt-out charismatics who have done everything once and now have no sensations left to experience.

## 12 Saturday jobs and exams

Because Christian parents are often keen to encourage the work ethic, studious habits and self-reliance, Saturday jobs and GCSEs may be taken very seriously indeed, to the extent where Christian activities suffer. The teenager may well gain the impression from his family that these things are a lot more 'real' and vital than anything you do at church.

## 13 Hesitation to do what you know adults want

When I was a teenager, I wanted to be baptized for ages. But I wouldn't admit it because I knew all the adults wanted me to! Giving in would have been handing over my freedom.

## 14 Uncertainty about salvation

Most churched kids can't point to a specific moment when they passed from darkness to light. And because they have never lived particularly sinful lives, they often can't see many ways in which Jesus has changed them. The results: they are unsure that conversion really has taken place.

## 15 Looking over the fence

Many churched young people feel obscurely that somehow they've missed out by never kicking over the traces. Wouldn't it be better to have more experience of life?

As you look at this list, you may start to feel, like me, that it's a wonder any 'churched' teenager actually makes it through to maturity! But thousands do – and you can help them get there. Here's how.

# 10-Point Strategy for Discipling Churched Youth

### 1 *Create a desire*

You won't turn churched kids into disciples by merely preaching 'you should' at them. They need to see in action an attractive example, of the kind of radical lifestyle you want them to take up. Your teaching programme needs to be designed with that in view.

You need to expose them to other groups where the kids are a little further on spiritually than your own. You need to take them to places (such as OMs 'Teen Street' convention, or similar YWAM activities) where they will meet young people of their own age or slightly older, who genuinely are sold out for Jesus Christ. Your personal example must reinforce your teaching; the way you live, set your priorities, spend your money and make casual conversation will communicate much more than a dozen Bible studies.

They also need to hear other teachers who are dynamic, uncompromising and yet attractive to teens in their style. Make full use of tours, weekends away, videos. Just keep exposing them to the possibilities until their hunger for reality starts to grow. And it will, if you back it all up with consistent sacrificial prayer.

### 2 *Look for Lydia, identify Apollos*

Some kids have an enormous influence on others. They are the opinion-formers in your group. Either (like Lydia) they will be gifted in bringing in others or (like Apollos) they will be full of unharnessed potential. Ask God to help you spot where they are. They are your key people; win them and you get the others; lose them and lose the rest too.

### 3 Form a core group

Get together those who really want to take discipleship more seriously. Start to pray together, to support one another, to explore New Testament principles of living. Take them away sometimes; a lot of growth can take place in just twenty-four hours away from home. Ensure the core group does not become a superholy elite; stress that any of the group can come along, but they have to accept the purpose of the core group and be serious about following Jesus. Encourage growth in the group. Allow those who are developing most noticeably to help those who are just beginning to come.

### 4 Emphasize practical action

Give them projects to carry out which will demonstrate love in action, sacrificial self-giving, whatever it is you are learning about. The last thing churched kids need is more unapplied doctrinal learning. Help them commit themselves in action to the concepts they are learning.

### 5 Stay in close touch

Become enough of a friend to be able to ring them up or get together with them in between meetings. Let your life make an impact on theirs. If that affects your social calendar, so be it!

### 6 Overhaul everything

Don't take their knowledge of the Bible or of Christian doctrine for granted. There can be surprising depths of ignorance in church-based kids and appallingly unchristian attitudes in their opinions.

Teach them to think Christianly and scrutinize everything in the light of the Scriptures.

There are particular things which usually need to be stressed. Many churched teenagers have a superficial faith and need to be taught about the primacy of a personal walk with God. They have a good scriptural basis of understanding and need to learn how to use it, to develop it into serious study of the Bible. Their grasp of apologetics can be weak (since they're not practised in seeing the world through non-Christian eyes) and they will need help in developing reasons for their faith.

They need to sort out their testimony and see clearly what God *has* done in their lives. They need to become positive about obedience in the family and participation in the fellowship. They need to learn to recognize their own emergent spiritual gifts. And they need a *lot* of teaching about how to live out their faith sensibly yet attractively in the outside world.

## 7  Point them towards the adults

As their hunger for God develops, teach them to feed on the resources available in the church fellowship. Introduce them to significant adults who can give them something valuable. Don't allow yourself to become the indispensable guru without whom their faith collapses!

## 8  Send them out to do things

Whether it's visiting other groups, sharing their faith on the street or taking on holiday projects abroad, keep them moving! Never allow them to settle into the view that Christianity is just a matter of weekly church attendance – all too common among churched kids. Build up their sense of adventure!

## 9  Teach them to support each other

Show them how to be caring and sensitive (too many churched kids

have competed unmercifully with one another in a most ungodly
way right through Sunday school!). Get them praying for each
other. Show them that they are responsible for each other's development (Hebrews 10:24).

## 10  *Realize your limitations*

There is a limit to the number of quality relationships any one of us
can have. The Lord spoke to thousands, but discipled only twelve.
Don't spray your work around ineffectively – concentrate on the
small number of key people with whom you can sensibly work.
They will reach the others for you if you are doing a good job with
them (2 Timothy 2:2).

I was a churched teenager, and at times I nearly gave up. But
today I'm grateful for the adults who never gave up on me. If you
have the privilege of working with Michaels and Lauras, go for it
with everything you've got. They may have been in the church all
their lives but they still need you if they're going to survive.

# Discipling Unchurched Young People

U nchurched young people might as well be on another planet as far as many churches are concerned. They're difficult to reach and even harder to keep. Time and money are usually spent on easier targets. That sums up the attitude in many British churches and chapels over the past twenty years.

During that time the Church has been putting most of its youth work resources into keeping the few young people it has rather than reaching the vast majority of children and young people outside its influence.

According to the 'Reaching and Keeping Teenagers' (RAKT) survey by Peter Brierley, published by the Christian Research Association (Monarch) in 1993, most young people in Britain – around 90 per cent – have no church links.

If a church is struggling to keep its head above water and cope with membership decline, working with groups of people considered to be difficult to reach or disciple is usually considered too much of a luxury. 'Softer targets' or the needs of the church members who are parents of teenagers get the scanty resources. But with the decline of central and local government funding to statutory youth work and the appointment of growing numbers of full-time local church youth workers/pastors, increasing numbers of churches are gearing up to reach unchurched young people again.

Many a church has bravely set a course to reach teenagers from the local estate only to come to a premature halt when the cost of reglazing the church-hall windows becomes prohibitive. But even if a church has conquered the challenge of remaining unfazed by spilt coffee on a newish church carpet or complaints from the caretaker about rowdyism, harder barriers lie ahead.

- What happens when unchurched youth make a faith commitment? Do you invite them along to church services and the church youth group? Or set up a special follow-up group just for them?
- How do you teach a book-centred faith to people from a non-book culture?
- How do you integrate unchurched youth into the adult church?
- Is it possible for these new converts to reach their unchurched friends without falling away from the faith?

Throughout the UK, Christian youth workers are grappling with these and a host of other issues as they try to give pagan young people opportunities to become radical disciples of Jesus. In my role as editor of *Youthwork* magazine I have talked to some of the youth workers who are breathing fresh life into old discipleship models and exploring exciting new methods to keep unchurched converts.

'We never plan an evangelistic event unless we have something set up for those who become interested in the faith,' says David Howell, a forty-something Baptist minister who has worked in the Swindon area as director of Thamesdown Youth For Christ since 1980.

'Also we don't get into the "what happens next?" without thinking beyond that, so we always keep one step ahead. If we fail to do this I think we are failing in our evangelism,' says Howell.

More and more youth workers and evangelists have adopted this approach, often as a result of the disappointment of seeing large numbers of young people respond at an evangelistic concert only to see them quickly disappear again.

In 1991 a youth church was launched in Swindon with the active support of several local churches, specifically to pick up on young people contacted during a schools mission. Called 'The Gap', its aim was to encourage 'interested' youngsters to make an intelligent decision about the faith.

A five-week follow-up course was run. After a year about eighty youngsters were still attending, most of whom were among the original one hundred and twenty who signed forms at the mission to say they were interested in finding out more about Christianity. Their successes and failures have helped to shape their current programme, structure and ethos.

'The first six weeks of "The Gap" were very evangelistic, but when most had become Christians we had to alter the teaching content,' says leader Greg Thorne. 'We also began to introduce worship and this gave us a problem which is ongoing – the programme tended to appeal to the regulars rather than newcomers. Although we tried to stay newcomer/not-yet-Christian-friendly, I'm not sure how successful we were.'

Three years later and most of the original group of youngsters are now eighteen. Some have been successfully integrated into local churches, others have left for college, a few remain and help to run the meetings.

'We decided "The Gap" should not attempt to grow up with them,' says Thorne. 'Instead we are targeting a new group of unchurched younger teens.' The learning process continues.

Heather Boyd worked her way up from volunteer to full-time paid director of Coventry Youth for Christ before leaving to study at London Bible College. She now works in Harrow, North London, as a middle- and secondary-schools worker employed by a cluster of local churches. Her youth work experience includes detached street work, schools work, visiting young people in prisons and local church youth groups and clubs.

'When I began discipling unchurched converts my assumption of what they knew was high. It took me a long time to realize that when they said they knew *nothing* about Christianity, they meant *nothing*.

'One guy once said to me, "Oh there was a geezer who died on a cross, wasn't there?" and that was the sum total of his knowledge of God and the Bible! You have to teach them everything – and you can't do that in a week. I had an agenda of what I wanted to teach them – assurance, sanctification etc. – but often they didn't want to know about that. They wanted to know about acceptance and self-worth, so I had to adapt my ideas about discipling when I began.'

Boyd also learned early that integrating unchurched converts into a youth group with churched youngsters isn't easy.

'Unchurched converts *might* be similar to the young people in your youth group/church, but most often come from very different backgrounds. You might be friendly and inviting. But if you are introducing them to a threatening situation, anything you give them that is positive is negated by the coldness and lack of acceptance from the Christianized youngsters.'

For several years Laura Johnson ran a Crusaders group for unchurched converts on a tough South London council estate as part of her job as full-time children's and youth worker in an Anglican church. She overcame the gap between unchurched and churched young people by taking them away on a holiday.

'The two sets got on brilliantly because they were all doing things they had never done before – abseiling and canoeing – where they all wore the same jogging suits and safety gear. They ate together and even slept in the same dormitory. When they returned home we noticed they would sit next to each other in church services, which would never have happened before,' says Johnson.

Apart from one parent of the 'nice' children who didn't want their son mixing with 'rough street kids', the rest of the church parents took a positive attitude to this mixing process. However, the churched and unchurched youngsters still continued to meet in separate midweek groups as their needs remained different.

The ten to fourteen group which Laura led was formed in a parish with tough council estates which suffer from a high crime rate and have very few facilities for children and young people. The group started by meeting for ninety minutes in the church hall for an activity evening which included team games and a fifteen-minute 'God slot'.

'The kids needed a lot of structure, otherwise they got bored and hard to handle,' says Johnson who was assisted by seven volunteers. After a year of this structure the youth workers took some of the regulars on a joint churched/unchurched weekend of adventure activities plus six God-slots.

Of the twenty-two young people that attended, fourteen made commitments and a group that met in Laura's home was set up to disciple them.

'The meeting consists of forty-five minutes of Bible study and then they stayed for tea – they were hard to get rid of,' says Johnson with a chuckle.

'Because of the low level of their reading skills, we could only get through five or six Bible references at most in three-quarters of an hour. It was a nightmare trying to get them into Bible-reading . . . I've given them Bible-reading notes, but I had to go through them beforehand giving them the page numbers, because they would never cope with just the book, chapter and verse.'

Despite the group being mixed sex, Laura was assisted by another female leader from the church.

'This wasn't such a problem to the young people,' says Laura, 'as ninety per cent were not used to men in their lives, coming mainly from one-parent families. Communicating "God as Father" was a bit of a nightmare. We asked them what they would like dads to be like, not the dads they've got or the floating male boyfriends their mum had. By actually asking what a dad should be like we started to look at the positive aspect of God as Father. Because they had some good and positive images of what males can be like (leaders at the open youth club) that helped. However, some of the girls especially found it hard to relate to males, and continued to be frightened of men.'

Unlike some churches, when the young converts began attending the main church worship meeting the adult members made them feel welcome and seemed genuinely pleased to see them around. They were given opportunities to take part in church services.

'The church was happy about integrating unchurched young people in principle,' says Johnson. 'As far as major changes in services go, that was a struggle, although we introduced worship services suitable for youth. The church was willing to give things a go.'

In the late sixties Terry Dunnell began experimenting with discipleship groups for new converts from an unchurched background.

'The young people would say to us, "Well, Jesus is great, but what has that got to do with the Church?" They felt they were being made to move away from their roots to conform to the manner, style, fashion and culture of the Church.'

In full-time youth work since 1966, Dunnell is Midlands field officer and spiritual development officer for Frontier Youth Trust, based in Leicester. Dunnell accepts that things have improved and increasing numbers of churches are learning to adapt to unchurched converts. However, he considers the major barrier is the cultural package we put around Jesus.

'Attitudes are changing, but they haven't changed anything like enough. If the RAKT survey is anything to go by, the Church has a long way to go.'

Halfway houses for unchurched converts are often set up as a result of the youth workers' frustration with the church. However, putting off the day when you attempt to integrate converts into mainstream church can sometimes merely delay the problem, not solve it.

In practice some discipleship groups appear to spend almost as much time on attempting to modify behaviour traits which might offend the adult membership of the church as on educating them about core doctrines.

Since many churches resist change, it is the unchurched young people who are expected to adapt to the culture preferences of the adult believers instead of the other way round.

'Suggesting that we need to strengthen young people to face up to church life is a terribly sad statement, but often it's true,' admits Heather Boyd, who works in London but is originally from Scotland.

'I believe you need to teach the basics about the faith to teenage unchurched converts and get them into fellowship with each other before trying to get them into the main church.'

When unchurched converts stick in a church, Boyd considers it is usually because of the quality of relationships they have formed. 'One lad who came from an unchurched background stuck in a local church because he was sociable and very acceptable. But he had a strong personality, he was outgoing and friendly and easier to love than many other unchurched converts.'

Andy Harrington, former director of Lincoln Youth for Christ, agrees that 'the average unchurched young person finds it hard to fit into a church – whatever the denomination'.

With the support of the churches in Lincoln, YFC under his leadership has set up discipleship groups which are more than just halfway houses but are not quite a youth church. It is their job to disciple new converts YFC makes through street work.

'Non-academic young converts need lots of experiential input,' says Harrington, 'but it needs to be firmly based in Scripture.

However, since most belong to a non-book culture, that doesn't mean we pull out a Bible every ten seconds. It does mean a lot of discussion, and the discipler needs to model the faith.'

Andy has now left youth work in England and moved to a part of the former Yugoslavia with his family to minister to youth in Croatia.

One of the most successful programmes to disciple unchurched youth in recent years continues to develop in a sleepy Dorset village. Although its pioneer, Johnny Sertin, has moved on and is no longer the full-time director of youth work in Canford Magna parish, in the four years he was employed by the local Anglican church in partnership with Youth With A Mission, Johnny set up a programme which saw significant success in terms of numbers of new unchurched converts discipled into significant levels of Christian maturity.

The youth work was based around a cell system – in 1994 the church currently had twelve groups with a total of one hundred and eighty young people. Most were unchurched.

Leaders needed to attend a twelve-week training programme, followed by a two-term apprenticeship before they could head up a cell group. Sertin told potential leaders they needed to commit themselves to a minimum ten hours' input a week to the youth work. As well as meeting as a small group twice a week, the group leaders were expected to meet one-to-one with each group member once a month – Sertin calls this 'fortywinking'. The groups have a minimum of six and a maximum of twenty.

'The monthly *fortywinking* is a crucial part of the discipleship strategy,' says Sertin. 'During that meeting the young disciple will receive a spiritual check-up and face questions such as: "What has God said to you, what have you said to God, what are you struggling with, and how have you found the means to overcome?" The leader will try to help them with their Bible reading and prayer life as well as build up the relationship.'

Formal teaching comes monthly in a meeting with all the cell groups together. Further input comes from informal and experiential teaching, ministering with the Holy Spirit. Although most of these small groups were aimed at mid-to-older teens, the church also run two cell groups for eleven- to fourteen-year-olds.

'We found that eleven to thirteens will do what they are asked to do and are very activities-orientated. From about thirteen to sixteen they become interested in themselves, discovering who they are. Then when they get past sixteen they want to do something about who they are and what life is all about. It's crucial that the church gives these older teens something to do,' insists Sertin.

'Many young people leave church because they feel it has nothing to offer them to do. We try to catch this group of potential leaders who can serve the younger age groups.'

The cell groups build social bridges to reach the rest of their people group. These groups are all single-sex.

'The advantage is that we can talk with them openly about sexual matters. Also with middle-teenage boys the attitude is very much "we are the lads."'

Sertin tries to remove the young people from what he describes as 'the merging points of the sexes – drink, drugs and sex'.

'It is helpful to find things that take them away from this. For instance the lads have these mad wild games in the woods in the middle of the night which we call male-bonding times. By comparison most of the girls would prefer to go somewhere and talk.'

John Wesley, the great eighteenth-century evangelist and founder of Methodism, developed single-sex discipleship groups of about six people who seriously aspired to holy living. Sertin's structure bears striking similarities to Wesley's methods.

Sertin built up a local profile and made contact with local unchurched youth through holding raves, other big events and having a drop-in 'doss house'. But latterly recruitment was mainly by the young people themselves.

One cell group which called itself the FBIs all went to the same school and they started a minicongregation which meets at the school on a Monday lunchtime. As a result several more girls were contacted, some becoming Christians.

'We want a holistic approach, we try not to segregate where the evangelism happens from where the discipleship happens,' says Sertin. 'Discipleship is evangelism, pastoring and teaching – I believe that is the Jesus model. If you don't do it that way you put the Christians into a ghetto where they have no access point to reach out any more.'

Another cell group was an Indie band called Prefix. Their aim was to break into the Indie people group with their music. So they have a reaching-out point, but they are also being discipled and cared for.

All the groups tend to orientate round an interest or age-group. 'We studied Jesus' methods of how he particularly identified his immediate group of disciples. We looked at how Jesus called them and gave them a purpose, but also in that context gave them an identity, relating to the fact that the initial band were fishermen, and how he related to an apostolic gifting that most of them had. I believe it is helpful that each small group has an identity oriented around gifting and whatever they are into. If we were successful it was because it has been *for* young people *by* young people,' says Sertin.

This last sentence is, I believe, crucial and should be underlined in red ink.

In a later chapter Tony Campolo comments in some depth about the importance of involving young people in practical ways and projects which help the discipleship process, a process he calls 'praxis'.

Empowering young people with the training, support and encouragement to get involved in 'working out their faith' and then actually releasing responsibilities to them is a principle many Christian youth workers believe in but fail, for various reasons, to facilitate.

We will also be examining the process of empowerment in the chapter on mentoring.

When asked whether it is becoming harder to disciple unchurched young people, all the youth workers I spoke to agreed that, while it has never been easy, it is getting harder.

'I just didn't realize the can of worms that comes up when you work with unchurched youngsters,' says Laura Johnson. Things like abuse, abortion, drugs etc, are becoming commonplace. You're not just having this nice, cosy Bible study, you are having to deal with some horrendous issues. As a result I became deeply involved in their lives. It is quite an awesome responsibility, which I didn't realize when I started.'

David Howell agrees: 'The amount of baggage that needs to be dealt with in a new convert has grown. These past hurts are often very deep, and it takes time and care before they can enjoy healing and wholeness. Another problem is the level of selfishness our society encourages in people. People are self-concerned and ask, "Is this going to be helpful for me?" But it is actually a selfless community that we Christians are called into. So as well as counselling and caring for new Christians I try to encourage them to get out and help care for others. That's sometimes the best way to cope with your own problems.'

After all the work, prayer and anxiety, seeing previously unchurched new Christians sharing their faith and showing loving concern for their peers has to be one of the most rewarding sights on this earth.

The fresh, raw, uncluttered language they use to describe the change God has made in their lives has a profound effect on Christian and non-Christian alike.

# Mentoring

On a March evening in 1966 I became a Christian. Aged just nine, I fully understood that the faith of my parents, sisters and brother was theirs, not mine, and I needed to have a personal relationship with Jesus Christ. I realized that although I knew quite a lot about God, it was based on second-hand information. I can still remember today the excitement and joy of the moment nearly thirty years ago when God arrived in me.

Between then and now a variety of people were to influence and shape my Christian experience. But without a doubt the most significant was my youth leader, Dave Hanks. During my teenage years he spent quality time with me teaching me formally in a Bible-class setting, and informally through conversations in a multitude of settings including during a round of golf and walking to and from watching Portsmouth Football Club.

Just as important – I was able to observe him in a range of situations. I have Dave to thank for my footballing and political allegiances as well as a more secure faith in Christ. Dave helped me to grow up in God. Often he was unaware of the impact his words or actions made on me. He was also quite honest with me about his own failings and humanity.

Although I looked up to him, I didn't hero-worship him in an unhelpful way because he didn't try to cover up his weaknesses. That was important. Since my youth I have been able to observe others who have helped nurture faith in young people. What they have in common is a commitment to influence positively young people – to help them in the transforming process of sanctification.

But I have also seen some who were regarded by young people as virtually perfect. When inconsistencies and flaws in their hero's/heroine's lives were exposed, some lost more than their respect for their youth leader/minister, they lost their faith too.

Being a mentor then carries huge responsibilities. But what exactly is a mentor? One of the most helpful books I have read on mentoring; *Connecting* by Paul D Stanley and J Robert Clinton (NavPress) 1992, defines mentoring thus:

> *Mentoring is a relational process between mentor, who knows or has experienced something and transfers that something (resources of wisdom, information, experience, confidence, insight, relationships, status, etc.) to a mentoree, at an appropriate time and manner, so that it facilitates development or empowerment.*

Stanley and Clinton also helpfully point out that there are a variety of mentoring types (*see* table) and that instead of seeking to use only 'ideal mentors who can fulfil the whole range of mentoring functions . . . if you narrow your mentoring needs to a specific area, you will usually find someone available to mentor' the young person who needs help in the area the mentor can relate to.

This table highlights the various different roles a mentor can perform. But even in the more informal types of mentoring it is important that mentor and mentoree talk about and agree upon the extent of the mentoring relationship and the goals that are to be achieved. In this way both parties share the same expectations of what the mentoring can achieve.

# Mentoring Types

| MENTORING TYPE/ FUNCTIONS | CENTRAL THRUST OF EMPOWERMENT |
|---|---|
| **Intensive** | |
| 1 Discipler | Enablement in basics of following Christ. |
| 2 Spiritual Guide | Accountability, direction and insight for questions, commitments, and decisions affecting spirituality and maturity. |
| 3 Coach | Motivation, skills, and application needed to meet a task, challenge. |
| **Occasional** | |
| 4 Counsellor | Timely advice and correct perspectives on viewing self, others, circumstances, and ministry. |
| 5 Teacher | Knowledge and understanding of a particular subject. |
| 6 Sponsor | Career guidance and protection as leader moves within an organization. |
| **Passive** | |
| 7 Model | *Contemporary* A living, personal model for life, ministry or profession who is not only an example but also inspires emulation. *Historical* A past life that teaches dynamic principles and values for life, ministry, and/or profession. |

Table from *Connecting* by Paul D Stanley & J Robert Clinton (NavPress) 1992.

In my opinion young people who are new believers mostly need one person to act as their intensive mentor – a friend who can be depended on to listen and offer a supporting shoulder. But they can also helpfully gain from having a second 'occasional' mentor who can provide specific input, training or support on a specific issue or area.

For the past year I have been spending time with a young person in what Stanley and Clinton would categorize as a 'teacher' type occasional mentoring relationship. Ryan (not his real name) has been a Christian for only eighteen months and comes from an unchurched background. In the short time he has been a Christian, Ryan has demonstrated that he is naturally skilled at relational youth work. I have also been trying to help him discover his other talents, some of which could include leadership skills. Part of this process has included questions aimed at helping him to analyse his own strengths and weaknesses and questions about his future career and vocation.

My role is to help Ryan discover his natural skills and also facilitate training so that he can fulfil the calling God may be putting on his life.

As well as conversation and prayer together we also work on a detached youthwork team. At present I am heading up the team alongside Ryan, but in time I hope to take more of a back seat while he takes over the reins. Within a measurable time span we have made goals which we are together working towards.

## JESUS-STYLE APPRENTICESHIP

Jesus employed an intensive mentoring method of relational teaching with his disciples. During his travelling ministry of three years, his followers were able to observe, listen to and model themselves upon Christ. Amazingly Jesus did not write a manual or 'how to' book on discipleship for his followers to use. Instead he depended on the mentoring process and the oral tradition used by contemporary Jewish rabbis.

In his excellent book *Mentoring For Mission* (Jensco/GEM 1992) Gunter Krallmann points out that Jesus' mentoring 'technique' was similar in many ways to the two strands of teaching adolescent Jews would have received as they grew up.

Boys were trained by their fathers into the family trade or business. Joseph then would have used this *vocational apprenticing* system with Jesus to teach him carpentry skills. Jesus would have spent many hours observing Joseph in the workshop chiselling, planing, measuring and sawing wood. But this apprenticing model was also well established in intellectual and spiritual training.

> The teacher-disciple relationship had already been observable in Greek society where Socrates, Plato and Aristotle each had their students and was a familiar phenomenon within Judaism as well. The rabbinic 'talmud' i.e. 'pupil, scholar, disciple', was seen as 'the one who gives himself as a learner to Scripture and to the religious traditions of Judaism . . . the pupils [while they sat around the rabbi] frequently engaged in debating theological issues, especially those relating to the proper interpretation and application of the *Torah*. Although note taking was practised, the instruction method was essentially oral, with a strong emphasis on memorization.[1]

A brief glance at the Gospels shows that many of the principles of *rabbinic tutoring* were also adapted by Christ as a useful apprenticing method.

Above all, by spending a lot of time with his disciples Jesus' teachings were not heard in isolation from the many opportunities his followers had to observe the implications of his teachings in everyday situations.

But as well as observing and listening, Jesus made sure the disciples had plenty to do. We know that some were assigned specific practical tasks e.g. Judas Iscariot took care of the money. Jesus also sent them off in small groups to preach and heal the sick and was around afterwards to debrief and pick up the pieces.

With patient and loving care Jesus moulded and so affected the lives of all but one of his closest followers, that they went on to make a major impact on the world. Many of them even died for the cause of Jesus who had become their friend, master and role-model.

## JESUS OUR ROLE-MODEL

'To this you were called because Christ suffered for you, leaving you an example, that you should follow in his steps' (1 Peter 2:21 NIV).

When the Apostle Peter wrote of Jesus being our example he used the Greek word *hupogrammos* which is its only use in the whole New Testament. Through contemporary Greek writings we know that this word refers to a method of teaching children to write. At that time papyrus, made from bulrushes was used as a type of paper. But papyrus was too expensive to be used for the early scrawl of children. Instead, Greek primary teachers used a shallow box filled with soft wax and a stylus. The pointed end of the stylus would scratch into the wax and when the exercise was complete the wax could be smoothed flat again. The teacher would engrave a line of letters or words with the stylus then the student would try to copy the letters and words below.

So Peter is saying: 'Just as the schoolboy learns to write by copying the perfect copper-plate example, so we are scholars in the school of life, and we can only learn to live by copying the perfect pattern of life which Jesus gave to us.'[1]

But there was another way of using the *hupogrammos* which has something to contribute to Peter's meaning. Quintilian in his *Education of an Orator* (1.1.27) tells us that sometimes the schoolteacher traced the letters in the wax of the tablet: and then the hand of the boy 'is guided along the grooves, for then he will make no mistakes'. At first the master helps the child by placing his hand over the scholar's, but then he let him try it by himself and the edges of the grooves kept him from 'straying beyond the boundary'.[2]

What a brilliant picture Peter has given us here of how Christ is our role-model and example. We should be copying Christ, closely following in his steps. Note that the context of this word 'example' is the suffering that Christ went through for us and that we will inevitably face if we become his disciples.

Jesus made it clear that 'If anyone would come after me, he must deny himself and take up his cross and follow me' (Matthew 16:24 NIV). When Jesus talked about taking up a cross, his disciples knew what he meant. Condemned criminals had to carry their cross through the streets to their place of execution. Carrying a cross meant pain, no turning back and usually death.

By using the word *hupogrammos* Peter is saying that we must copy Christ's pattern of life and death. Without seeking out suffering or persecution we should be stoical, patient and calm in the suffering that following Christ is likely to bring.

The picture of the wax tablet and stylus also lays down a good principle of mentoring that the teacher/youth leader/mentor must have a life worth copying, and that at first the mentoree will be more reliant on the mentor before gradually gaining confidence, learning and becoming more mature.

This last point is important. Our task is not to produce clones of ourselves but disciples of Christ.

Intensive mentoring may involve opening your home to someone, becoming their best buddy, sharing your life, a virtual adoption sometimes!

To help avoid some of the potential dangers and abuses inherent in opening yourself to this extent, it is vital that you avoid the cultivation of exclusive mentoring relationships. The mentoree should also spend time with other members of the Christian community and clear measurable goals within a timespan should be set. The mentoree should understand that in time the intensity of the spiritual growth programme will slacken as the mentoree takes more personal responsibility for his/her own walk with God. The mentoree in turn should want to mentor others and pass on what he/she has learned.

Peer education is making a growing impact in several areas, most notably in sex education and HIV/AIDS awareness programmes. Most young people gain the majority of their information or mis-information from what their peers say and do. If we are to see the revival-scale numbers in church growth among young people that we long for, we need to equip, train and release young people into peer evangelism and peer nurture.

## EMPOWERMENT AND TRAINING

As his disciples grew and developed in their faith in him, Jesus gave them ministry responsibility. Empowering young people is an important part of the mentoring relationship and one where many come to grief. Empowerment requires giving young people some area of responsibility having trained them to handle this area without major disaster.

All too often churches and youth workers provide one of these elements but not both. Giving a person responsibility without providing him/her with the tools to do the job is highly destructive. If you give a group of youngsters the responsibility to plan the programme for the next month at the youth group without preparing them for the task they are likely to fail. They need to be shown the options, given resources, maybe taken to different youth groups to see different models and styles of programmes. They need to be shown ideas books, they need to be trained in the process of brainstorming, praying and reaching compromises together in the decision-making processes of programme planning.

With this sort of empowerment the young people will be able to mix their creative ideas and original concepts with what they have seen, heard and read elsewhere. Without it they are likely to fail, causing stunted self-esteem and shattered confidence.

Likewise, being trained and empowered with this information and training only to discover they are not actually going to be given the power to decide or influence the programme is destructive and very frustrating.

Empowerment requires responsibility and training in joint measure to work properly.

Many youth workers can relate easily to these points as they themselves have not been fully empowered by their churches/ church leadership. In most churches and denominations the power structures rest mainly with men aged between forty-five and sixty-five. I know of a church where a large group of mainly twenty- and thirty-somethings were asked by their church leaders to attend a series of leadership training meetings. But at the end of the course there was nothing for this group to do beyond their existing roles. All the training did was raise expectations of responsibilities and influence which were not given.

This frustration which many youth leaders feel can be usefully used to help us understand how many young people must feel who have not been empowered. Frustrated youth leaders must ensure that they do not inflict on the next generation of Christians what has been inflicted on them. By learning the lessons of church history, *you* could help to break the chain of failure to empower, but this is only possible if a generation of new leaders have a servant attitude towards leadership instead of grabbing and then fiercely holding onto power.

That is why you and I must look at the influences and positions we currently have and before God hold them lightly and be actively empowering the next generation.

1 *Mentoring For Mission* by Gunter Krallmann (Jensco/GEM) 1992
2 *New Testament Words* by William Barclay (SCM) 1980, page 139

## 9

KATHY HOLKEBOER

# Discipling by Design

'Lord, what am I supposed to do with Emily?' I prayed. 'She's so sweet and so eager to please. But I don't know *how* to teach her to apply principles from the Bible.'

I had tutored Emily in algebra, and I knew it wasn't easy for her to apply concepts to practical situations. She needed to see things more concretely. Now she had asked me to help her study the Bible.

Struggling with how to teach Emily reminded me of others I had tried to help in the past. I love word studies using Greek words, but a teenager I discipled was not impressed. She wanted an example of how the concept would work in her life.

Another youngster wanted to skip the illustrations – just be given the concept. And now I was faced with Emily, who survived algebra only be memorization.

Suddenly I was reminded of the *Learning Style Inventory*[1] I'd taken years before. This inventory reveals the different ways people approach learning.

For example, some learn best by listening to a lecture while others learn through hands-on situations. The Lord seemed to be saying to me that I should disciple Emily with her particular learning style in mind. The *Learning Style Inventory* I was familiar with defined four basic styles. Actually, there aren't just four (or even 400) learning styles. God has created each of us with unique gifts and abilities. Some of us have a blend of several learning styles.

Yet, keeping individuality in mind, we can gain insight into the best ways to disciple others by meeting four classic personalities.

Part of our investigation will include examples of how Jesus taught different kinds of learners as well as ideas as to how to communicate spiritual truth to a particular learning style. Let's start with Carol, the Concrete Experience learner.

## CONCRETE EXPERIENCERS

The Carols I've known are delightful. They love people. They use their feelings and the opinions of others to make decisions. Grasping theoretical principles behind a concept is usually difficult. They learn best from being involved in specific examples and they learn from each other better than from an authority.

When Emily, a Carol type, asked me to study the Bible with her, I knew that giving her the task of identifying basic scriptural principles in a passage would be outside her best method of learning. So when I tried to teach her what Scripture says about gossip, I used a 'finish the story' approach. Her assignment was to read this story:

> Once upon a time there were two friends. George was always quiet and contemplative while Fred was usually bouncy and bubbly. Fred could never understand George's silence and assumed George had something to hide. One day Fred shared with Peter the assumption that George (the quiet one) had a secret sin. Peter was shocked to hear about George, and he told Mary, George's boss's wife, that George was a pyromaniac . . .

After writing her end to the story, I asked Emily to check it against Proverbs 16:28 ('gossip separates close friends'), and Proverbs 17:9 ('whoever repeats [a] matter separates close friends').

The method worked. After finishing the assignment, Emily related a situation at work where she had misinterpreted someone's comment and passed it on as truth.

Concrete Experience learners need real examples to understand scriptural principles. Studying the lives of biblical characters provides excellent examples for them.

The parable of the Good Samaritan (Luke 10:25–37) is an example of how Jesus communicated spiritual truth to empathetic, people-oriented learners.

## ACTIVE EXPERIMENTERS

Another learner with slightly less people-orientation is Alex, the Active Experimenter. Typically, Alex learns by doing! An Alex seems to learn well if he can verbalize his thoughts in a small-group discussion or if he is allowed the freedom to work on a project.

Basically, he will learn best in an active, 'hands-on' situation. Being part-Alex myself, I know what it's like to listen intently to lectures but not clearly understand the concepts until I've done the homework. In fact, I have a hard time gaining much spiritual input from listening to sermons. But when I explain the content to someone else, it becomes clear to me.

Alex would have relished the opportunity Jesus gave the seventy-two evangelists in Luke 10:1–17. Jesus sent them out two by two to announce that he was coming. They were given authority to heal, and they came back rejoicing that even the demons were subject to them in his name.

How would an Active Experimenter learn scriptural principles about gossip? Preparing to lead a Bible study on gossip would probably help him most as he would discover the principles himself during this hands-on activity.

One Alex I know was effectively discipled by a very wise Christian worker. She was willing to risk letting me lead a Bible study and be a leader in student ministry after I had been a Christian for only three months.

Because I learn by doing, preparing to lead a Bible study forced me to gain much more Bible content than I would have as only a participant in the study.

## ABSTRACT CONCEPTUALIZERS

Alice, the Abstract Conceptualizer, learns well when someone in authority has directed the learning. If there is something to analyse or a theory to comprehend, she's eager to learn it. I knew a sixteen-year-old Alice who had to know the why behind everything. When I discussed the Bible with her, she would develop her own theories and even draw diagrams to explain her point of view.

On one occasion, Carol, another student told Alice she was wrong about a biblical interpretation, even though the other student couldn't explain why to Alice's satisfaction. I sent them both home with an assignment to read several chapters in Romans. After Alice systematically analysed God's authoritative word, she commented, 'That wasn't fair – you picked the passages to support Carol's view.' Even though she didn't want to admit her theories didn't line up with Scripture, she did face the truth after careful, analytical, systematic investigation.

An Alice usually forms firm opinions, with or without expressing them. To gain God's perspective on the topic of gossip, she could do a verse-by-verse study that would reveal God's view on the subject. However, the instruction to do the study should leave room for Alice to develop her own creative approach to the topic. The Pharisees in Matthew 19 may have been learners like Alice. They wanted to learn in authority-directed, systematic packages. Since their opinions were well established, Jesus knew he would have to quote their authority, Moses, in order to be heard.

# REFLECTIVE OBSERVERS

Not all learners are motivated by the why of things. Reflective Ryan prefers a lecture so he can take the role of impartial, objective observer.

Reflective Observers are usually introverts. Since they rely heavily on careful observations to make judgments, we shouldn't expect them to be quick thinkers.

I asked one Ryan why he didn't seem to be growing spiritually.

'I don't know,' he said.

'So, does that mean, you don't care?' I countered.

'I don't know,' he said again.

I was an Active Experimenter trying to disciple a Reflective Observer. I was asking for an immediate, spontaneous response from someone who needed time to think before he could adequately respond.

If I had asked the question and given him some time and further input, we probably would have had a good discussion about his spiritual growth.

In this particular situation, time proved extremely important. When he was ready to let God begin working in his life, he asked me for tapes of a speaker we had heard at a conference two-and-a-half years before.

Reflective Observers benefit from small-group Bible study when homework is required. Doing the Bible study before they come to the meeting gives them time to think.

At the meeting it's important to let them sit quietly. They learn as they listen and will probably make significant contributions if not pushed.

Probably the best way for Ryan to gain God's perspective on gossip would be to assign him to take notes on a lecture about gossip. The more respected the speaker, the greater the impact. Jesus used the lecture method frequently, most notably in the Sermon on the Mount (Matthew 5–7).

# A COMBINATION OF STYLES

Perhaps thorough learning requires equal amounts of all four styles. But each of us tends to learn best in a unique blend of one or more of these styles.

As for the Christian youth worker, God will place young people in our paths who want to learn. We need to know them well enough to provide a learning environment best suited to each one.

- Carol, the concrete experience learner, needs to be involved with people in real situations.

- Alice, the abstract conceptualizer, wants analytical explanations of concepts.

- Alex, the active experimenter, learns best as he does something.

- Ryan, the reflective observer, needs to read and think over a period of time.

Remember Emily, the Carol type we met at the beginning of this feature? Over a period of many months, she eagerly did the Bible study homework I'd designed specifically for her, she matured in her faith and became active in the church.

One Mothers' Day during a sharing time in the worship service, she expressed her appreciation to women in the church who had been 'mothers' to her. I was encouraged to hear my name mentioned.

I'm convinced my relationship with her would have been entirely different had I not discipled her according to her unique learning style.

## Practical Discipling Strategies

### Concrete Experiencer
*Spontaneous role-play*: Provide enough structure to make your point, but be prepared to discover other issues as you go along.

Chitchat that *seems* unproductive may create a learning environment for this type of learner.

*Small-group or panel discussions*: Ask people to share their experiences and then be open for questions.

## Active Experimenter

*Agree-disagree discussion*: Prepare a statement that is somewhat ambiguous and have people state their reasons for agreeing or disagreeing.

*Field trips*: Arrange opportunities to see ministry in action – homeless shelters, crisis pregnancy centres, behind-the-scenes work at a mission or youth camp etc.

*Surveys:* Send them to neighbourhoods in pairs to gather opinions on religious topics or to the church congregation for opinions on social issues, etc.

*Projects*: Participate in a building project for a local charity; prepare a dramatic presentation (and ask a Concrete Experience person to star in it!).

## Abstract Conceptualizer

*Personal Bible study*: Character studies allow Conceptualizers to use their analytical skills. Word studies requiring research of the original Greek or Hebrew words can be effective for the more able Conceptualizer.

*Writing Poetry*: Have the learner express in poetry or some other written format what he/she gleaned from studying Scripture.

*Diary/journal*: Writing a 'letter to God' after reading Scripture provides an excellent learning exercise.

*Inductive study*: Teach the Conceptualizer how to take apart a passage verse by verse, find the spiritual principles and apply them to real situations.

**Reflective Observer**

*Lectures*: Good quality sermons and youth-group teaching slots work with this learning style.

*Demonstrations*: Show how something is done without asking for participation.

*Book reports*: A report on an interesting book will probably encourage an Observer to read the book.

*Tapes/radio/films*: Listening to good speakers on tape or radio and watching videos give the Observer a chance to think.

# Crunch Questions

On Your Own

1 Recall times you have enjoyed learning spiritual truth. Did you learn by:
   (a) discussing the topic with others or seeing an example of the principle in action? (Concrete Experiencer)
   (b) participating in a hands-on project or explaining the concept to someone else? (Active Experimenter)
   (c) doing your own Bible study? (Abstract Conceptualizer)
   (d) hearing a speaker? (Reflective Observer)

Which one or two of the learning styles in the article best describe you?

2 If you are currently in a house group or other setting for learning that is not suited to your learning style, how could you supplement the teaching/instruction with activities that would better help you to grow spiritually and understand the material?

3 Think about the times you have enjoyed communicating spiritual truth, either in a small-group, one-on-one, or up-front setting.

Describe the learning environments you created.
Which types of learner would respond most positively to your methods?

4 Think about the young person(s) you are helping grow spiritually. What type of learner(s) are they? Suppose you want to teach those person(s) about the effective use of time. What might be some effective ways to help them learn?

5 Pretend you are leading a small group containing young people of all four learning styles. You want to teach them about the effective use of time. How would you construct a lesson that would be meaningful to everyone in the group? Describe the format you would use, advance preparation you would assign, activities the group could do and how you would wrap up the session.

For discussion with other youth leaders/workers: to which of the four learning styles are most discipleship groups for young people geared? How could a youth worker modify the group time so that the content would be meaningful to people with different learning styles?

1 *Learning Style Inventory* by David Kolb (Boston: McBer & Co, 1976, rev. 1985, 137 Newbury Street, Boston, MA 02116, USA).

## 10

Tony Campolo

# Praxis What You Preach

## Community

It is in community that we become human. Who we are and what we are – these are created in the context of the intimate relationships that community provides. Sociologists from George Herbert Mead to more recent proponents of small-group theory have pointed out that it is by viewing ourselves from the perspective of the significant 'others' in the dominant primary groups in our lives that we come to understand our identities and our purposes in life. Our values emerge from primary groups that have the power to establish for each of us a prevailing worldview.

When community is lacking in our lives, we seek it desperately. In our vulnerability we are even willing to join strange and destructive groups. That's why cults are springing up all across America, Europe and beyond. People are driven by deep social-psychological hungers that can be gratified only in intense community.

The effects of intense community became all too clear when we saw the unfolding events with the Branch Davidians outside Waco, Texas. As individuals chose to leave that cult's besieged compound early in the confrontation, we expected that they would emerge confused and glad to be free from their totalitarian guru, David Koresh.

Instead they presented themselves as true believers who saw themselves as part of an elect group of God's people ready for the *eschaton* (Second Coming). There were no signs of disorientation in their demeanour and they radiated a self-confidence that was far from evident in the opposing government agents who were supposed to be in control of the situation.

These Branch Davidians knew who they were and what their lives were all about. The cult provided identity and meaning to these members who conveyed a sense of having ultimate meaning to their lives as they presented themselves to the waiting press corps.

## COMMUNITY GONE SOUR

Community provides what popular experts in the field of the sociology of religion call a 'plausibility structure'. This is a worldview and theological belief system that stands over and against what is considered reasonable in the dominant society that surrounds the community, but is taken-for-granted truth for community members.

Thus it seems reasonable to men in the community to give up their wives to the leader of the community and for mothers to advise their teenage daughters to sleep with him. In a community discouraged from interacting with the rest of the world, a short-sighted logic comes into play that makes what is abhorrent seem right. Almost any world philosophy can be maintained if it is sufficiently reinforced by the plausibility structure of the primary group.

In a more limited sense, gangs provide the same things for their members. Ever since Frederic Thasher did his classic study of gangs, sociologists have known that membership of a gang meets many of the emotional needs of alienated youths in urban settings. Those without meaningful family ties who live in a society that has lost its way often find a sense of belonging and a system of order for themselves within a gang context. In the gang they find norms to live by, albeit norms antithetical to what society in general defines as right and wrong.

US sociologist Milton Yinger argues that we cannot really understand gang membership except in religious terms. He believes that gangs provide the sense of community that people in the Church often talk about, but seldom provide. Gangs provide a setting in which teenagers can find something to live for – a code of behaviour that defines how they should live and an identity that gives them personhood.

## PRESCRIBED ANSWERS

There was a time when such desperate commitments to gangs and cults were unnecessary because young people found community in the extended family. Before the urban/industrial revolution, people lived in social systems made up primarily of blood relatives, a structure classically named *Gemeinschaft* (German for 'community'). For the most part, social units within the system were cut off from daily interaction with non-members. What youngsters did with their lives was prescribed by the community and one's identity was a clearly defined gift from the group. Life outside the 'blood brother' ties of such a group was unthinkable. Young people never had to ask such questions as, 'Who am I?'

Freedom, of course, is out of the question in such arrangements. Whether in a real *Gemeinschaft* (an isolated Tasidi tribe in the jungles of the Philippines) or in what sociologists call a pseudo-*Gemeinschaft* (the compound of the Branch Davidians), the total lack of freedom is a prominent feature. Loss of freedom is the trade-off for the security and meaning that the community provides.

Most of us think freedom is too high a price to pay for community. That's where we're wrong, however. The prominent psychoanalyst Erik Fromm clearly showed that for most confused teenagers who float in a state of normlessness, freedom is a burden they readily relinquish.

They don't have to be coerced into giving up freedom; they look for a place to lose it. The *pseudo-Gemeinschaft*, be it a gang or a cult, graciously takes freedom off kids' shoulders. No longer must teenagers make their own existential decisions. Identity and meaning, cast out of the realm of individualistic choices, become instead prescriptions of community.

Community life need not be like this, though. There is the possibility for something else. In the Bible it's called *koinonia* – the community of faith that Jesus envisioned when he called Peter to be the one on whom he would build his church. Our Lord had in mind a community encompassing freedom of choice without loss of security or identity – a group that would celebrate the individuality of its members.

Some sociologists contend that such a group cannot exist. You can't have your cake and eat it, they argue. These social scientists point out that, in the realm of social reality, community produces an either/or situation. They maintain what one writer calls 'an ambivalent attitude' towards community. Community is valuable for its prescription for identity and its provisions for security, they concede, but in the end these sociologists prefer the freedom that is found in the mass society of the modern urban world. They accept the blessings of modernity but not without a wistful, nostalgic glance back at the *Gemeinschaft* of the past with all of its blessings.

To our sophisticated colleagues in the field, we Christian sociologists have some good news – the gospel. We believe a community that provides both identity and freedom *is* possible. What's more, that kind of community has happened from time to time. That's what church is – a happening. That sense of belonging, wherein we find out who we are and in which we can live and move and have our being, comes upon us from time to time.

While we can sometimes find church within the institution that bears its name, however, we cannot make *koinonia* happen through social engineering. Like the apostles of old who broke bread with Jesus after walking with him on the road to Emmaus, only *after* the event do we realize that we have had the shared ecstasy that makes community into communion. But it does happen. To those who fail to see it because they confuse the religious institution with the sense of community that sometimes happens to its members, we can only say, 'We have this truth in earthen vessels.'

Theologies and sociologies can be quite abstract, and youth workers demand something that has more flesh on it. Good news! Help is available. Interestingly enough, insight into how youth workers can foster community comes from a sociologist spurned by many in the evangelical tradition – Karl Marx. Sometimes those who do not walk with us can help us see things that we ourselves do not see because we are too close to them. Such is the case with the Marxist idea called praxis.

## LEARNING FROM IDEOLOGICAL ENEMIES

Those who are initiated into the field of sociology readily recognize the concept of praxis, and those who are conversant in liberation theology are no strangers to it. In simplistic terms praxis is a special kind of reflection that occurs in the context of action. The revolutionaries who joined in the Marxist causes believed that it is in the struggles for freedom that true humanity is discovered. During the tensions of conflict with oppressors the oppressed become comrades who find what their lives are all about and who they really are.

Don't write off this leftist ideology too quickly. Those who cannot learn from their ideological enemies are doomed to the stagnation that comes to all who think they have the final word. I argue that the youth worker who invites the young people in the institutional church to engage in the struggle for love and justice in society may well be surprised by *koinonia*. I watched such things happen between black and white Christians who joined hands in the Civil Rights movement. I saw it happen to Christian groups who refused to stand on the sidelines during the Vietnam War.

More recently I saw *koinonia* happen at my own college among those who joined together in a campaign for gay rights. Eastern College came to that time in its history when homophobia and discrimination against gays would not be tolerated. Jokes about lesbians were no longer considered funny and hints of gay bashing were opposed with vehemence.

Don't be mistaken: Eastern College forbids same-sex coital relationships. Eastern College president Roberta Hesteness has stated that she won't tolerate either homosexual behaviour or any forms of discrimination against those who have homosexual orientations.

I watched gay and lesbian young people who had hitherto lived in closets come out. I observed with joy as persons sick with bitterness and resentment over what they had endured showed miraculous signs of healing. Most of all, I saw heterosexuals and homosexuals discovering *koinonia* in a fellowship committed to ending the oppression of gays and lesbians that haunts most Christian college campuses.

It happened! The praxis community was created. I saw people who didn't even like each other come to love each other in a common bond of faithful commitment. I watched people who had never prayed meaningfully find in their shared ecstasy the capacity to pray. In the conflict that seemed everywhere evident on campus, many found the freedom to be what God had called them to be as persons – and did so in the context of a loving community who shared a common allegiance to Christ.

Our gay brothers and sisters gave a sigh of relief. They realized they would have to live according to an understanding of Scripture that prohibits homosexual behaviour, but they revelled in the victory they gained in ending discrimination. In the struggle they had found themselves as individuals as well as discovering the excitement of community.

# CHURCH MEANING GETS BLURRED

Praxis need not occur in the context of such controversy, however. A group of young people on a work project with Habitat for Humanity discovered community as they built houses for hurricane victims in south Florida. Working together all day and then reflecting on their shared experiences in the context of action provided them with a second conversion. They discovered the meaning of church.

I head up a missionary effort that brings hundreds of college students to Philadelphia and Camden, New Jersey, each year to work among some of the most socially and economically disadvantaged kids in America. These short-term missionaries spend each day during the summer months working with teenagers and children for whom the term 'at risk' is an extreme understatement. As they struggle to help boys and girls overcome the oppression of the socioeconomic system and the devastation of family life, they do more than they are able to realize at the time. In helping children and teenagers come to know Jesus in a personal way, even in the midst of such social insanity, they discover community and identity. Each evening as they reflect on what has happened during their daytime conflicts, they realize and renew their calling. They sense their purpose in life. They experience Jesus telling them who they are. In praxis they learn community.

All of this can lead to but one conclusion: community is an absolute necessity for those teenagers whom we would reach with the gospel. In community, teens enter into a plausibility structure that can enable them to maintain their faith in a society that discounts it. In community they are able to find the security that enables them to bear witness for Christ to their friends at school and in the marketplace. In community they can assert, 'I know in whom I have believed and am persuaded that he is able to keep that which I have committed unto him against that day.'

To be a youth leader is to be called to foster community. You cannot create it, 'because the spirit bloweth where it listeth, and you cannot know from whence it comes and whither it goeth.' But you can make your youth ready for community. You can open them up to the receiving of the Spirit who makes them one. You can invite them to share in the action that leads to the transforming reflection that makes people new.

In attempts to create community in the not-too-distance past, youth workers created a religious equivalent of secular minority groups. What we learned is that after all that touchy-feely stuff was over, there was often a void. *Koinonia* rarely happened. We thought that community could be created simply by having the youth group put their chairs in a circle and really relate. Most of us were disappointed. Now the call is to discover community in praxis. The cynic has every right to question whether or not it works. I submit that I have seen it.

## PRAXIS MAKES PERFECT

Tony Campolo's contention that he has *seen* community in praxis would find an affirmation from youth leaders who have indulged in the challenge of Christmas Cracker. There can be few youth projects that have so successfully provided an environment for the expression of community.

The fostering of community is an important goal for the youth worker. Perhaps this is one reason why Cracker has been such a catalyst for action: the national staff includes people experienced in youth work.

Project director Richard Wood ran an 'Eat less, pay more' restaurant in Worcester in 1989 before becoming involved with the national operation. A youth worker by profession, Richard quickly realized Cracker's potential:

I was excited by the way Cracker provided a framework for Christian youth groups to both exert an influence in their locality and do something positive to contribute to a global issue.
Here was a relevant project which actually let young people off

the leash, allowing them to express their faith and their creativity as individuals while knitting together in their bid to help the needy.

Cracker has greatly impacted many local communities as businesses, schools, media and the Church work together in partnership. Whether it be Radio Cracker, Crackerterias, 'Eat less, pay more' restaurants or Alternative Christmas events, Cracker's inventive approach has given youth leaders ammunition to focus young people's attention on a major task – and achieve it.

Cracker helps young people begin to grapple with Third World development issues through positive action. The project has proved the potential young people have to offer in what Campolo labels 'the struggle for love and justice'.

Cracker upsets our 'ignorant bliss' and goes a step further. It actually helps create those who can be 'significant others' so that, as young people from outside the Church begin to work alongside Christians, community becomes a field for evangelism. Christian young people are excited to be seen as leading the pack for once, to be striking out with a project that captures media attention, that allows them responsibility, that encourages their input. Their confidence in knowing they are speaking out because Jesus is concerned for the poor is built up. Conversely, the non-churched young person sees a unity and commitment that is inspirational, and a structure that both encourages togetherness and draws out individual creativity. In short, a community of Christians in action.

Christmas Cracker may not have been set up by Oasis Trust and *Alpha* magazine as an evangelistic project *per se*, but it has become so very naturally as those involved have gone about their task.

For further information about Christmas Cracker, contact:
Christmas Cracker Trust, 5 Ethel Street, Birmingham B2 4BG.
Tel: 0121–633 0873. Fax: 0121–633 0875.

## 11

PAUL BORTHWICK

# Young People and Mission

I n response to the freedom he experienced on a mission team, sixteen-year-old Wayne returned home and sold his television! 'I saw how much time I was wasting watching TV,' he explained.

When asked what was the most valuable aspect of the team, fifteen-year-old Debbie reported, 'I got into the habit of either memorizing a verse or having a quiet time every morning.'

The idea of such lifestyle changes may not readily spring to mind for the average youth worker facing his or her lazy, pleasure-seeking youth group who have OD'd on TV the night before. But yes, it is possible to disciple young people. And yes, they do respond positively to a mission or service opportunity.

Unfortunately, the terms discipleship and youth ministry are seldom linked. Many see youth ministry as an intermediate phase, a sort of 'holding pattern' in the spiritual growth of a teenager in which we attempt to keep the student out of trouble and in the church until he or she, at age eighteen or older, can make an intelligent commitment to Jesus Christ.

This vision of youth ministry is unfortunate for two reasons. First, it cheats youth leaders because it reduces them to baby-sitters or entertainers whose top objective is to keep the junior or senior highers busy. Second, it cheats young people because it concentrates on their immaturity (and tends to perpetuate this immaturity) rather than their vast growth potential.

So how can youth be discipled? How can the youth leader go beyond the 'fun and games approach' to youth ministry? How can this vast potential for growth be tapped in the teenagers with whom we work?

There are many tools which are being developed for such discipleship with youth. For our purposes, however, I would like to focus on the idea of a short-term mission project as a tool.

My premise is this: short-term mission projects, properly executed and led, are the best opportunity in youth ministry for the discipling and development of youth as leaders and as growing people.

My basis for this premise is eighteen years of intense involvement sending youth and adults on over one hundred short-term mission teams. We send teams out on one-to-four-week projects. The teams travel cross-culturally, ranging from other settings in our own country (US) to Africa, Europe, Latin America, the Caribbean, and on one occasion, Asia.

Youth teams have built houses, painted buildings, dug wells, led 'Backyard Bible Clubs', preached at churches, led in evangelistic campaigns and any number of other ministries.

We now offer these teams for adults. But our focus is still youth, with over 60 per cent of our teams being designed specifically for teenagers.

Many of our projects focus on physical labour (painting has been our forte). We keep the ratio of leaders to students consistent at about one to four and the team size is kept small at ten to fourteen. We initiate and set up most of the projects by contacting the mission agency, local host organization or church.

Administrative planning for these teams begins between nine and twelve months before the project, although some (like a building project in Burkina Faso) can take two years to plan, while others (a trip to Trinidad after a coup in Haiti forced us to cancel two weeks before departure) have been put together in a matter of weeks.

To maximize growth in our team members, we exhort students to begin praying about involvement as long as eight months before the project. In March, an official presentation of the project opportunities is made, and in April we begin to accept applications and the teams are formed.

The training takes place in May and June, because almost all of our team projects occur over the summer months of July and August.

Preliminary application requirements for the project include the following:

a) a written testimony

b) a financial deposit

c) parental permission

d) a commitment to fulfil the team requirements.

If a student meets those requirements, we accept that student onto the team with an 'official' acceptance letter. If he/she cannot meet the requirements, then we investigate the reasons. We try to go out of our way to make it possible for a student to participate.

If the student cannot write the testimony, it is usually because of lack of assurance about personal faith or because of a lack of understanding of what it means to be a Christian. In our experience, a number of students have made personal commitments to Jesus Christ through such investigations.

After initial acceptance onto the team, a student is then given the team requirements. Those requirements include:

a) Scripture memorization

b) a geographic/cultural report on the area/culture to which the team is going

c) team meetings (at least four) in which details and plans are discussed, a team unity is built, a spiritual foundation is set, and some cross-cultural education takes place

d) an appearance before the church missions committee

e) raising the remaining finances

f) reading a missions-oriented book

g) participation on a Team Training Retreat (three days and two nights where the teams work, eat and live together as part of their preparation for service elsewhere)

h) formulating and adherence to a Team Covenant, an actual 'contract' that team members write concerning their growth goals, service priorities and commitments to community on the team

i) participation in a team commissioning service (in which they will recite their Scripture and be sent out by the laying-on-of-hands by church leadership)

j) completion of a number of assignments and readings in our 'Team Training Manual'

k) a commitment to report back to the youth group, church and school about their mission experience.

Additional requirements include the recruitment of prayer supporters, attendance at 'How to Paint' (or some other skill) seminars (conducted by a painting contractor) and application for financial aid to our Missions Committee (as needed). On some occasions, team preparations have included fund-raising activities and local, community outreach as part of the requirements.

Regarding the basic premise of discipling youth, we consistently observe that student interest and participation in these projects have increased in proportion to the number of requirements. Our first team had fewer requirements, but as we have progressed, we have demanded much more of those who want to go on these teams. Their zeal to serve has been in direct relation to the amount that has been demanded of them. If students are made to pay the

price (in fulfilling the hard requirements), they tend to value the
service project much more.

## DEVELOPING LEADERSHIP

The premise is carefully worded, 'properly executed and led'. The
reason for that is obvious. When projects are sloppily executed
or led by those who are ill-equipped to work with teenagers, the
results can be disastrous. To find those who will do best as leaders
for such teams, we look for leaders with the following qualities and
characteristics:

1  Administration ability – at least one of the leaders on a team must be
   a detail person. There will be a myriad of little details (especially on
   the international teams!), and if these are not cared for, the team will
   function poorly and opportunities for discipleship may be lost.

2  Rapport with teenagers – some of our team leaders are in their
   twenties and others are in their fifties; age neither guarantees nor
   negates success with youth. The key ingredient is ability to listen to,
   understand and enjoy teenagers. The person who has a great zeal
   for missions but who has a short temper with those who giggle, talk
   after 'lights-out' and turn their noses up at a sardine-spread
   sandwich will not fare well on a youth team.

3  Spirituality – we can only teach others that which we have learned
   ourselves – Jesus taught this in Luke 6:40. If youth mission projects
   are to maximize the potential of discipling the youth who are
   involved, the leaders must be established  in their own spiritual
   growth.
      The markers of spirituality for which we usually look are
   consistency in quiet times, a solid understanding of Christian
   doctrine, commitment to discipling others through relationships and
   leadership by example – a pace-setter who models Christian
   lifestyle.

4  Adventure – it is entirely possible for a leader to have all of the
   characteristics listed above without any desire to venture out in

cross-cultural service. A person may be a great administrator, a gifted leader of teenagers, and a man or woman of God, but if he or she will drop dead at the sight of a tarantula, it may be better that he or she not lead a team to the Tropics.

The leaders of a mission team can excite the students about the wonderful new things which will be learned on a team experience. If the leaders take on the new experiences as an adventure from God, the student will most likely follow. If, however, the leader is very timid about new experiences, a substantial part of the learning process may be thwarted.

We find that the best people to lead youth mission teams are those who have worked with our teenagers throughout the year. The adults who have an established rapport and relationship with the youth are more likely to be able to utilize the intensity of a mission team to the fullest in terms of discipleship.

## DISCIPLESHIP RESULTS

The preparation of both students and leaders for our youth teams has had the best results of any aspect of our youth ministry in terms of discipling our youth and building them in Christian qualities.

Leaders have grown out of students who, on first impression, would have been written off as dormant in their spiritual lives. Many parents have commented, 'We sent our teenager off as an immature youth and received him back as a growing young adult.' Where has the growth come? In the development of our students, we have seen measurable growth in the following areas in most of the summer team participants.

*Quiet times* – the idea of a personal, daily devotional time is familiar to many church youth, but few would claim much success in this area. Two-week projects have enabled us to create a controlled environment where there is a set time each day for this devotional exercise.

Students have learned how to make entries in a daily journal (a requirement on many of our teams), and they have experienced a degree of consistency in their prayer life and Bible study.

In other evaluations (we have done post-project evaluations since 1979), when asked, 'How did you grow spiritually?', most students listed the habit of daily quiet times as the primary way that they grew.

*Character development* – the intensity of these work projects has given us tremendous ability to see students grow in depth of character. Because of stress, new environments and the exposure to people who have very different kinds of lives, students have grown in respect of endurance, flexibility and thankfulness. We teach our students the difference between Western values and Christian values by letting them see the fact that not all Christians are the same, look the same or worship the same. The cross-cultural education has helped students develop their personal priorities; one stated, 'I see how much time I spend shopping; when I saw how poor some people are, I began to rethink my habits. Owning a lot of "things" just isn't as important to me any more.'

It should also be noted that many parents have noticed a growth in the diligence of their youth as a result of teams. Many teenagers, especially those under age sixteen, have never experienced a forty-hour work week. When we work on these projects, we work at least that much, and many students are stretched into realizing their own potential as workers.

*Personal responsibility* – perhaps the best maturity factor that has come as a result of these youth teams is the way in which students have grown with respect to being responsible for themselves.

From the outset – with the preparatory requirements – to the close of the project, students are reminded that they are both members of a team and persons responsible for themselves.

Students learn that their behaviour directly affects the success of others. If they fulfil their requirements, the team benefits. If they are lazy in their work, the team suffers. Although some would disagree with this, we have allowed students to go off shopping on groups of two or three in foreign countries. Our underlying philosophy has been: 'If we treat students like adults and give them responsibility, they are more likely to respond as adults.'

*Leadership* – the responsibility learned and the experiences of youth mission projects have had a wonderful effect on our youth group. Of the more than one hundred students who have gone out on teams over the past three years, over 50 per cent of these are involved in some sort of leadership in our youth group.

As a result of seeing the success of their team on a project, the youth have returned with a deeper commitment to serve in the leadership of the youth ministry. The mission teams have given students a feeling of responsibility – the resulting feeling that 'we fulfilled our responsibility there' has led to increased willingness to undertake responsibilities here.

The positive effect of doing these service teams has assured students that God wants to use their lives, and that assurance has given many of them courage to be used by God in our youth group.

*Witness at school* – it is sometimes stated that those who want to be missionaries abroad should first be witnesses at home. This is true, but on our youth teams we have found that the opposite has also been true – those who have gone out on teams (many of whom would never speak out about their faith before they went) have come back with a new zeal to share Christ with their friends at school.

The reasons? Perhaps the deeper commitment which a project requires has had corresponding effects in boldness to witness. Perhaps the exposure to missionaries has given students more understanding of the need to proclaim Christ. Whatever the cause, the effect has been more students who are sharing the love of Christ with others.

The project requirements suggest that students, after the project, talk about what they have learned with their peers. This reporting back mechanism has taken on various forms. One student did a report in a geology class on 'Erosion in the Yukon'; as a result, he was asked why he went, and he shared with his fellows the basics of missionary service.

Another student produced a slide show for her sociology class based on her 'missionary' experience in the inner city of Newark, New Jersey. As a result, she had an opportunity to share her testimony, and then she was invited to show the production to two other sociology classes!

*Servanthood* – as a result of these teams, many of our students have learned a deeper sense of what it means to serve others. The work they have accomplished on the teams has often been of the 'behind-the-scenes' variety, and this has taught them the importance of all the work done in Christian ministry which goes unnoticed and unappreciated.

The team emphasis on our projects has taught students how to care for each other. It has been a beautiful experience to watch students care for those who get sick, and through the course of a project, everyone gets an opportunity to serve as an encouragement and an uplift to others.

The lessons of servanthood have been transferred to home environment as well. Students have learned the importance of serving the members of their own family through the 'family' experience provided by the team.

In addition, there has been a marked increase in students' willingness to take on the obscure tasks in ministry – a factor which we attribute to the mission teams.

*Worldwide Perspective* – those who work with youth may find it easy to become frustrated with the narrow-sightedness of teenagers. For youth, today's crisis – whether it be an exam or a new pimple – tends to dominate their thinking.

We have been refreshed to find that those who have gone on teams have gained a healthier perspective on the world and on their individual lives. Their perspective on God has enlarged as they have seen new lands, new people and new ways to serve God. As a result, the everyday problems which they confront have seemed less significant.

This worldwide perspective has also resulted in a greater desire on the part of our students to submit to the Lordship of Jesus Christ, especially with respect to his call on their lives to consider cross-cultural service.

Some of our students are headed towards missionary service. Others are not sure, but they are opening themselves to the call of God. The exciting dimension of this worldwide perspective is that students become more informed about and committed to the work of God throughout the world, and they start to see their lives in that respect.

### Where do you go from here?

Suppose you are now willing to consider a short-term mission team for your youth, a team which will be part not only of a missions outreach but also a defined part of your 'leadership development' programme. What should you do?

Several immediate ideas:

### 1 Consult existing resources:

*Youth and Missions* by Paul Borthwick (Victor/Scripture Press) £7.99.
*Youthwork* magazine (Aug/Sep 1995 issue) contains a comprehensive listing of mission agencies which provide short-term missions/service opportunities in the UK and abroad.
Christian Service Centre produce an annual updated *Short-Term Service (STS) Directory*, phone 01902 882836 for more details.

**2  Consult other youth workers or churches who have had experience:** Contacting other churches who have sent youth teams is a good idea because their feedback offers a 'reality check'. They can tell you how some of the principles in this article worked (or did not work) on their teams.

**3  Look for service opportunities:** 'I want to do this, but where can I take my youth group?' is the most common response question from youth leaders. Don't wait for an exotic chance to paint the Taj Mahal or repair the Great Wall of China. Look for practical, cross-cultural opportunities close to home – a home for the elderly, a neighbourhood church serving people of a different ethnicity from your own, a shelter for the homeless.

**4  Look for hosts who believe in the vision:** The greatest results on these teams come when the hosts believe they are also part of the discipleship process. Hosts who see the youth team as a form of cheap labour will have a neutral or negative impact on the youth.

On the other hand, hosts who believe that the primary purpose of the team is to change the lives of the participants will contribute greatly to the growth of all involved.

Short-term mission projects, properly executed and led, are the best opportunity in youth ministry for the discipling and development of youth as leaders and as growing people. If your ministry priorities include the changing of young peoples' lives, youth mission teams present a possibility that you will not want to miss!

# Postscript

My son, Adam Wesley, is now two. He has just celebrated his birthday. Two years isn't very long and although he's a fast learner there are a multitude of things left for him to discover.

Two years also happens to be the average length of time that most Christian youth workers in the UK stay involved in youth ministry. In that short period of time many get discouraged or burn out. Worse, others treat youth work as a stepping stone to more 'important' ministry! It is a minority that stay involved and committed to youth work for longer than two years. But since experience, consistency and long-term commitment to building relationships with young people are so valuable, it is men and women who aspire to becoming youth ministry veterans that Christ and his church need.

That was a major reason why in 1992 Elm House Christian Communications, who I work for, launched *Youthwork* magazine. We wanted it to inspire, resource and above all encourage Christian youth workers to see their ministry not just in the short term. The fact is that no matter whether you are just starting out in youth ministry or if you are a seasoned veteran of many years, you need to look after yourself if you are going to continue to be used by God to show His love to young people and nurture them in the faith. And for me the single most important element that, while not guaranteeing against disaster, will provide a strong defence, is *living honestly*.

By that I mean that we must practise what we preach. When I tell a young Christian that it is important to pray, read the Bible and meet with other Christians, I need to be following my own advice.

We are all disciples of Jesus no matter how long we have been following him. Discipleship must start with you and me. We need to keep working at our relationship with Jesus, that is our first priority, and more important than making time to be with young people is our commitment to love and worship God.

Being Christian youth workers who consistently year in and year out serve young people as they live Christ-like lives must be our goal. With the power God makes available to us through the Holy Spirit, this is not an impossible dream but the legitimate demand God places on our lives.

Many happy returns, Adam. And many happy returns in youth ministry to you, I sincerely hope.

# 13

# Discipling Resources

Little more than ten years ago the British Christian youth worker would have had few discipling resources available to help him/her. But this is no longer the case. The wide variety of help imported from the US, together with a growing range of materials from the UK, mean that many people are just not aware of the choices on offer.

Between the writing and publishing of this book additional books, videos, activity packs and curricula will have been produced which aim to help the Christian youth worker nurture young believers. However, the following helpful list will provide you with a good starting place for browsing through the range of materials produced and written about. The chances are you will still need to adapt even the best materials so that they work for the particular group of youngsters you work with, but don't think that no help is available. Check it out!

NB This selection is a personal recommendation and is not comprehensive. A visit to a Christian bookshop well stocked with youth ministry resources is very worthwhile. Prices where given may differ.

## BOOKS

Nick Aiken, *Being Confirmed* (Marshall Pickering) £3.99
Aiken, a former diocesan youth officer, presents a down-to-earth

summary of the basics of the Christian faith. Useful for those contemplating confirmation within the Anglican church.

Nick Aiken, ed, *Creative Ideas For Youth Evangelism* (Marshall Pickering) £3.99
Includes ideas to help the youthworker train young people in evangelism, then lists a range of achievable evangelism ideas.

John Allan, *Just Looking* (Bible Society) £7.99
Five sessions look at: Jesus – who was he? Jesus' mission – was it a failure? Christianity – can you be sure it's true? Being a Christian – what's it like? The Church – Christianity's worst advert? Each session includes icebreakers, worksheets, group activities and is Bible-based. Great material for use with enquirers. At the time of writing, Bible Society announced a follow-up 'Just Starting' course.

Patrick Angier, *Faithbuilders* (Marshall Pickering) £7.99
Includes all the basics such as setting up the meeting place, peer ministry on handing over the reins, relationships, teaching ideas, projects, and activity/worksheets. A bit basic, but a good introduction.

Patrick Angier, *Junior Youthbuilders* (Marshall Pickering) £6.99
A range of teaching sessions, projects, socials, theme events, talks, games, quizzes and worksheets for use with eleven to fourteens.

Mike Breen, *Outside In* (Scripture Union) £6.95
Subtitled 'Reaching un-churched young people today' this is a must-read book if you are working or want to work with unchurched youngsters. Breen's innovative methods include identifying key people in whom God is working and nurturing faith in young people. Other chapters include sections on communication,

developing a total approach, making contact with young people, worship and pastoral care.

John Buckeridge, *Youthwork Ready-To-Use Meeting Guide* (Vol 1): *Christian Basics* (Kingsway) £6.99
Ten ready-to-use meetings which include teaching, Bible investigation, photocopiable sheets, related games/activities and optional extras around the themes of: discovering faith, sin, God the Father, Jesus, the Holy Spirit, the Church, the Bible, prayer, forgiveness and doubts. Designed to be used with new believers and not-yet Christians, three other ten-week courses complement the first volume; (Vol 2) *Lifestyle* looks at daily implications of being a Christian, e.g. resisting materialism, sex, independence; (Vol 3) *Culture* looks at pressures young Christians face, e.g. peer pressure, adverts, drugs; (Vol 4) *Beliefs* looks at doctrine, e.g. atonement, apologetics, second coming.

Rick Bundschuh and Tom Finlay, *Teach Toons* (Youth Specialties/ Zondervan) £6.99
These fifty meeting plans for eleven to fourteen year olds each include photocopiable cartoon worksheet. Design medals for your church members, put tattoos on the arms of St Paul's shipmates, and draw Peter's changing expressions as he steps out across the lake to Jesus – great fun!

CPAS *You'd Better Believe It* £4.95
Ten meeting plans on Christian doctrine including: sin, the Cross, the Resurrection, Heaven and Hell. Some sessions are quite heavy and require good literary skills.

Steve Croft, *Making New Disciples* (Marshall Pickering) £7.99
Identifies the route to spiritual maturity and offers guidelines and exercises for step-by-step growth in our Christian experience and

understanding. Not specifically a youth ministry book, but contains many useful lessons which apply directly to nurturing youth.

Pete Gilbert, *The Teenage Revival Kit* (Kingsway) £3.99
A meaty paperback for teens who are serious about Christian commitment, with practical advice on spiritual gifts, prayer, evangelism, etc. Follows up on his excellent earlier book *The Teenage Survival Kit*.

Peter Graystone, Paul Sharpe, Pippa Turner, *Yoyo 1–4* (Scripture Union) £3.95 each
Best used with younger teens/pre-teens these four books provide ideas for complete meetings including games and talks. The first in the series examines the image that Christians present and challenges the notion that Christians must be boring.

Andy Hickford, *Whose Life Is It Anyway?* (CPO £5 plus p & p)
This beginner's guide to Christianity includes separate notes and colourful worksheets for eleven to fourteens and fifteens plus leaders' notes. Additional worksheets are available at £1.40 each for the set. The notes for the eleven sessions are comprehensive and cover all the subjects you would expect e.g. Bible, prayer, assurance, mission.

Stephen D. Jones, *Faithshaping: Youth and the Experience Of Faith* (Judson Press) £6.95
The American author's concept of nurturing goes well beyond helping youth to make a one-time decision for Christ. He sees nurture as a process for helping youth grow in faith. Jones also examines evangelism theology and identifies stages in the 'faith cycle' as well as calling for youth workers to help build memorable faith experiences and help youth shape their culture.

Gunter Krallmann, *Mentoring For Mission* (Jensco/Globe Europe) £4.99
This remarkable book details the manner of Jesus' own vocational training and rabbinic tutoring in religious studies, and highlights the way the adult Christ used these same principles in mentoring his disciples. Not specifically aimed at youth workers, the principles in this book do apply to youth work and I recommend it highly.

Ralph L. Lewis and Gregg Lewis, *Learning to Preach Like Jesus* (Crossway Books)
Not strictly speaking about discipling/nurturing, I include this book because it contains vital information on inductive communication which youth workers need to adopt. The American authors examine the content and style of communication Jesus used and suggest ways we can and should replicate Jesus' preaching. Thought-provoking and readable, this book is a must for all youth communicators.

David Lynn, *Talksheets* (Youth Specialties/Zondervan)
This excellent range of American books provides a meeting outline and a photocopiable 'Talksheet' which provokes thought and discussion. The full range numbers six and covers Junior High (eleven to fourteen), Senior High (fifteen plus) and Parent Talksheets which aim to encourage interaction on the meeting theme between student and parent.

Phil Moon, *Young People And The Bible* (Marshall Pickering) £6.99
A mixture of methodology and ideas including meeting outlines which are strongly Bible-based. The content is oriented towards middle-class, easily motivated, 'Christianized' young people.

David Ng, *Youth In The Community Of Disciples* (Judson Press)
£4.99
Short but sweet this 79-page book(let) draws together some important arguments. American author David Ng outlines strategies for
encouraging teens to find their place within the church.

Arlo Reichter, *Get Away* (Bible Society) £4.95
The definitive book on residential youth work. If you want to take
your group away for a weekend or longer this is the book to read.
Practical 'how to' section on planning and safety aspects, plus a
range of weekend programme outlines and ideas.

Duffy Robbins, *The Ministry Of Nurture* (Youth Specialties)
A landmark book on nurturing faith in young people from one of
the United States' foremost youth specialists. Drawing on his large
youthwork experience Robbins outlines a thorough, flexible discipleship programme.

Paul D. Stanley and J. Robert Clinton, *Connecting* (NavPress)
Subtitled 'The mentoring relationships you need to succeed in life',
this book helpfully identifies a variety of mentoring styles and highlights their strengths in a very readable style.

Pete Ward, *Worship And Youth Culture* (Marshall Pickering) £5.99
An honest account of how a group of young people from Oxford
set up 'Joy', an alternative service for unchurched young people.
Provides key pointers on the importance of fellowship groups,
avoiding the 'getting high on God' mentality, involving young
people and the need for a relaxed leadership style.

Pete Ward, Sam Adams and Jude Levermore, *Youthwork And How
To Do It* (Lynx) £8.00
Helpful chapters include: exploring youth culture, working with
groups and interpersonal skills.

Mike Yaconelli and David Lynn, *Tension Getters* (Bible Society) £4.95
These fifty scenarios will trigger discussions on a wide range of subjects including prejudice, trust, peer pressure and pornography. Practical guidelines on facilitating discussion are included.

## VIDEOS

*Edge TV* (Youth Specialties/Scripture Press) £14.99
This growing library of issue-oriented videos from the US is available through Scripture Press in the UK. Typically each video is segmented into vox pops, music vid clips, interviews and true-life stories. Fast-moving with brilliant MTV-like graphics, this series is of a high standard and comes with good leaders' notes. Subjects covered include: addictions, self-image and sexual choices.

*Geronimo* (Scripture Press) £19.95
This 68-minute long film focuses on five inner-city gang members who are sent to a Christian camp by the court as part of their parole conditions. Their camp counsellor is a white middle-class back-slidden Christian. Superb performances from the young actors will keep unchurched teens watching, while there is a strong challenge to churched Christians too. Lots of humour, street talk, rap and a conclusion that lacks the usual clichés.

*Good Question* with Steve Chalke (Scripture Union) £9.99
With a variety of London locations as a backdrop, Steve Chalke explores the relevance of Christianity today. Designed for people who are asking questions about the Christian faith, this video is ideal for 'Just Looking' type groups of mid-to-late teens.

*Hands On: Making Confirmation Count* (CPAS/National Society) £49.95

A ten-session discipleship course with video and twenty photocopiable resource sheets comes with a wealth of other ideas to select and adapt. The video consists of short, punchy items related to each of the ten units.

*Make Love Last* (CARE Trust) £42.45

This 30-minute video was made primarily for fourteen- to fifteen-year-olds, for use in Personal, Social and Health Education classes at school. The mix of vox pops with young people, comments from experienced educators and gut-busting humour shows teens that saying 'no' to premature sex is a positive and rewarding choice. Designed to communicate to unchurched teens, the video comes with very extensive leaders' notes, and despite the high cost this video is well worth getting.

*Speak For Yourself* (Scripture Union) £14.99

In three sections of 12 minutes each, six older teens/early twenties Christians explain in short sound bites what God means to them, how they came to faith, and the difference being a Christian has made to their lives. An excellent discussion starter which will work best with older teens who are seeking faith or new believers.

*Paradise Road* (Scripture Union) £14.99

This four-part video-soap provokes discussion about moral issues by the cast of six late teens/early twenties who live together at 7 Paradise Road, a fictional house in London. Issues raised include premarital sex, lying and self-esteem. Comes with an excellent leaders' guide.

*Youthwork* magazine provides year-round ideas, resources and help for youth workers/leaders.

*Youthwork* is the magazine for all Christians actively involved in youth ministry. Edited by John Buckeridge, this bimonthly magazine contains practical ideas and resources for youthworkers/leaders including:

- Ideas – Games, discussion starters, theme nights, ready-to-use meetings, evangelistic projects.

- How Tos – Practical and comprehensive 'how tos' on the nuts and bolts of youth work.

- Youth Trends – Youth culture trends identified and analysed.

- Pastoral Issues – Counselling teens in crisis, accountability to church leaders, young people and the law etc.

- Resource Review – Latest books, videos, music reviewed in each issue.

- Headscratchers – Articles to make you stop and think through the theory and practice of youth ministry.

- Artworks – Photocopiable graphics in each issue.

Obtain *Youthwork* from your local Christian bookshop or subscribe by calling our Subscriptions Hotline 0181 942 9761 (Monday to Friday 9 a.m. – 5 p.m.).